cyber junkie

cyber junkie

escape the gaming and internet trap

kevin roberts

HAZELDEN®

Hazelden
Center City, Minnesota 55012
hazelden.org

Library of Congress Cataloging-in-Publication Data

Roberts, Kevin J.
    Cyber junkie : escape the gaming and internet trap / Kevin J. Roberts.
        p.   cm.
    Includes bibliographical references.
    ISBN 978-1-59285-948-1 (softcover)
    1. Video game addiction. 2. Internet addiction. I. Title.
    RC569.5.V53R63 2010
    616.85'84—dc22

                                                                          2010019853

Editor's note:

The stories in this book are true. Names, locations, and other identifying information have been changed to protect confidentiality; in some cases, composites have been created.

The information, ideas, and suggestions in this book are not intended as a substitute for professional advice. Before following any suggestions contained in this book, you should consult your personal physician or mental health professional. Neither the author nor the publisher shall be liable or responsible for any loss or damage allegedly arising as a consequence of your use or application of any information or suggestions in this book.

14 13 12 11 10   1 2 3 4 5 6

Cover design by Percolator
Interior design and typesetting by Percolator

To my mother.
You have always believed in me.

contents

Foreword   **ix**

Acknowledgments   **xi**

Introduction   **xiii**

Chapter 1   Welcome to the Cyber Universe   **1**

Chapter 2   Choose Your Poison   **29**

Chapter 3   Your Brain in Cyberland   **47**

Chapter 4   Into the Black Hole   **61**

Chapter 5   Climbing Out of the Hole   **95**

Chapter 6   The Journey of Recovery Continues   **115**

Chapter 7   A Guide for Loved Ones   **139**

Resources   **169**

Notes   **175**

About the Author   **183**

foreword

Only in recent years have we realized how prevalent addictions are in our modern society. We have progressed in our awareness from the abuse of alcohol and other substances, through countless sexual practices that may leave us both bereft of satisfying love and/or with profound feelings of shame, and we're now discovering new ways to bedevil ourselves with behavioral addictions, such as compulsive shopping or gambling.

Kevin Roberts herein adds another behavioral addiction to this growing list. Of greater importance is his success in taking us inside the mind of an addict. There we can develop both empathy and foreknowledge as we read explicit details of how people can become addicted in the cyber world.

Some may laugh, saying that nowadays everything is being labeled an addiction. Yet a reading of the first few chapters is likely to change one's mind, as Roberts takes us in heart-wrenching detail through the progression that left him a true addict. He also gives us a window into the cyber world to appreciate its vast and multifaceted appeal. We gain a valuable perspective into a form of recreation and communication that captivates tens of millions.

Essential to recovery is to talk with rigorous honesty about one's own struggles, and Roberts admirably demonstrates this practice throughout the book. In addition, the author shows how common it is becoming for cyber activity to lead to true addiction—something probably unsuspected by many who become addicts. Forewarned is forearmed.

I have personal knowledge on this subject. Since my retirement, I have spent lots of time playing bridge and solitaire games on the computer to soothe feelings of anxiety and shame. It's a short-term fix, which makes matters worse in the long run. Roberts's book helps me to see the consequences of this behavior when it becomes compulsive. And calling it by name—an addiction that "medicates" unwanted emotions—is a potent way of reducing its power to control our lives.

Like many addicts, I have traded one addiction for another throughout my life. I've struggled for fifty-five years with compulsive eating. I used food to cover up unpleasant feelings and constant anxiety. For the last twenty or so years, I have learned to resist my addictive food impulses by bringing the situation into the light of honest examination and even lighthearted humor, just as Kevin Roberts does in this remarkable book.

John Everingham, Ph.D.,
editor of *Men Healing Shame: An Anthology*
and *Breaking the Shackles: Bringing Joy into Our Lives*

acknowledgments

I am blessed with many friends who supported me in writing this book.

- Tom and Ann Houston, for tireless efforts in editing and challenging me to become a better writer

- Nathalie Shamma, for her eagle-eye editorial skills

- John Everingham, for editing some chapters and convincing me that I could do it; also, for being a powerful mentor these last ten years

- my family, for blessing me on my journey and always encouraging me

- Tony Vicich, for inspiring me to reach for my dreams

- Tim Kowalski, for believing in me when I needed it most

- David Wolfe, for convincing me that I was a writer

- high school English teachers Bill Petrovich and George Duffourc, for inspiring me to push past my literary limits

- Fr. Ned Donoher, for igniting and empowering my creative mind

- Tim Batdorf, for leading the way with his own book

- Terry Shulman, for offering valuable advice when I started the book

- Sari Solden and Geri Markel, for supporting this process early on

- Doug Rutley, for catching me in the act of a gaming binge and scheming thereafter to get me to acknowledge my problem

- P. K., for kicking my butt to be productive and helping me structure both the book and my time

- A.S., for awakening dormant parts of my self

- Barb Evangelista, for being a steadfast friend who always offers me honest feedback

- Maureen and Elektra Petrucci, for being loyal friends, creative consultants, and fellow cultural creatives

- Ryan Isakow, for offering me a teenage perspective on gaming and constantly encouraging me in this endeavor

- Andy Carter, for helping me to appreciate the inner workings of World of Warcraft

- Andrew Luginbill, for showing me the lighter side of gaming and sharing many insights on his own gaming

- Lambrini Makris, Christos, and the folks at Monty's Grill, for providing me with inspiration, support, and a place to write these many years

- all the folks I have worked with professionally, for trusting me with their stories

- and finally, thank you to all the following people, for helping me navigate through the depths of my issues: Ralph Johnson, Walter Clemens, Mike Dokuchic, Paul Soczynski, Bill Kauth, Charlie "Emir-Gandalf-Carlo-Brother Lawrence" Lewis, Barb Evangelista, Wayne Hicks, Palmer Stevens, and John Everingham

introduction

The Western world is in the midst of a cultural shift. Electronics and the Internet have transformed the way we live. Just a decade or so ago, devices such as computers, cell phones, and iPods were relative luxuries that made our lives easier or entertained us. For most people, these items are now nearly indispensable in both their work and their personal lives. The Internet and video gaming, likewise, are no longer used primarily for research or for occasional amusements. More and more, they are our main source of recreation.

For many people, video and computer games and other forms of digital technology are harmless. They offer convenience or a way to relax or have fun with friends and family members. Unfortunately, all of these devices also carry the potential to become addictive.

Users or players sometimes become compulsive in their use of these technologies. They may game excessively, turning away from family, friends, and the other activities they once enjoyed. Or they may become ensnared in social networking to such an extent that their forays into the cyber world become substitutes for real human contact. Facebook, Twitter, MySpace, online chat engines, and simply surfing for information can turn into all-encompassing obsessions. Relationships, health, and jobs may all suffer as a result—and yet the behavior continues. Though users may be highly intelligent and creative, they turn their backs on reality, absorbed in a world of imagination and fantasy. I used to be one of these people.

Video games and many Internet activities have taken their toll on my mental, physical, and spiritual health. Excessive playing and Internet usage have given me carpal tunnel syndrome and persistent back pain. They are the primary factor in missed appointments and have even cost me jobs, not to mention a whole lot of money. They have been a significant barrier that has gotten in the way of friendships and relationships. I have chosen video games over virtually everything and everyone close to me. I would chat all night online with "friends" all over the world instead of going out with friends in the here and now. For much of my adult life, video games, and then later the Internet, assumed a place in the forefront, inexplicably drawing me away from social outings, dinners with friends, and even time with my family.

Video games and the Internet are not the problem, however. I am the problem. I do not blame these industries. I blame myself. I loathed myself in those moments when I would finally emerge from a video game flurry. In those times of reflection, I would wonder how I could possibly have been so weak as to fall under the gaming spell once again. The disgust would rise up within me, and I would swear to myself that I had learned my lesson. I would rid the house of all games. I would resolve to quit chatting online. But eventually, the urge would resurface and overpower my best intentions. There's no other way to describe it: I was a video game addict, a cyber junkie.

Today, I am proud to be in recovery. I wasted years of my life staring into a computer screen, failing to achieve the goals I had set for myself. Although I felt pangs of guilt and sadness after gaming binges that lasted for weeks, it was not enough guilt to get me to stop. I hid my gaming from everyone for almost ten years and was in denial that I even had a problem. In 2003, I finally hit bottom and realized my life was out of control. I needed to make a change.

My road to recovery was long and hard, and I repeatedly relapsed into gaming. Playing video games heightened my senses, making me feel totally alive, while Internet chatting with friends around the world allowed me to unplug from the difficulties of my real-world relationships. It is not surprising that I suffered for years with cravings. Sometimes, they still haunt me. Through therapy, friends, and support groups, I have managed to stave off the cravings and stick to my recovery plan.

A few years into my recovery, I began working to help others learn how to escape from the claws of gaming and Internet obsessions. I befriended fellow cyber addicts and tried to offer the kind of support that my friends had offered me. My assistance was informal at first, but slowly I began to organize and facilitate support groups for cyber addicts. Today I run numerous such groups for people whose lives have been swallowed up by their insatiable urge to game, surf, and chat online. These groups offer the support addicted individuals need to turn away from compulsive behavior within the cyber world, which empowers them to channel their energies in positive directions.

This book grew out of my journey through cyber addiction. Throughout the book, I recount my personal experience, describing how an innocent pastime turned into fifty-hour gaming binges and all-night online chatting, and how I found a new focus for my life that did not involve these obsessive activities. I also share stories about people I have helped professionally. The experiences described in the book are real, though names and identifying information have been changed to protect privacy. In a few instances, I have combined stories to form composite characters.

Although I have vast personal experience with a variety of games and Internet activities, I needed to augment my understanding through research. To this end, I visited gaming forums and talked with players from around the world. In addition, I delved deeper into Facebook, MySpace, and other such networking sites, and I studied professional literature on the science of compulsive behaviors and addiction.

This is a book for anyone affected by overuse of the Internet, video games, or other electronic devices. The problem may be your own and you're struggling to understand why this is an issue for you and how to solve it. Or the problem may be with someone you love, a partner or child perhaps. That person may realize his or her activity is a problem; on the other hand, the person may not give a second thought to how much time and energy he or she is spending online and/or gaming. Cyber addiction is a new phenomenon, and thus, the research on the topic is limited but growing.

Here's what you'll find in these pages:

- Chapters 1 and 2 take you behind the scenes and enable you to peer into the cyber world. You will come to understand the allure of games and the Internet as well as attain a broad understanding of the different types of video games and cyber activities and the kinds of people drawn to them.

- Chapters 3 and 4 take a scientific and behavioral look at addiction, revealing how excessive Internet use and video gaming exhibit many of the telltale signs of addiction. A list of warning signs that your cyber use may be spinning out of control is also included, as are stories of others who have spiraled down into cyber addiction.

- In chapters 5 and 6, I recount stories from my recovery process and those of addicted individuals with whom I have worked. I also discuss relapse and how to create a healthy relationship with technology that adds to the quality of your life, not subtracts from it.

- Many readers are likely at wit's end trying to help a loved one who overuses technology. Chapter 7 can help family and friends understand how best to help a loved one who is a cyber addict, whether that person is a child or an adult.

You are about to embark on a journey into the cyber universe. Keep an open mind, and remember that there is nothing inherently wrong with playing video games or using the Internet. However, some people—like me—can't help but engage in these activities in unhealthy ways. The good news is that it doesn't have to be that way—recovery is possible. To help us, you must first understand us. I hope that this book provides that understanding.

CHAPTER 1

welcome to the cyber universe

"Understanding can overcome any situation, however mysterious or insurmountable it may appear to be."
Norman Vincent Peale

The phone rang, and I initially didn't answer. The caller was persistent, however. I finally decided to pick up because the ringing was breaking my gaming concentration. I had told all my friends that I was out of town, so I couldn't imagine who it might be.

"Hello," I barked into the phone.

It was Doug, a friend of mine since childhood. He and I had grown up on the same street, and he had recently started renting a room in my next-door neighbor's house. Doug declared, "I am fully aware of what's going on over there."

"I don't know what you're talking about," I righteously asserted as my right hand continued to work the computer mouse (I had turned down the volume to avoid detection).

"Well, you might have had me fooled into believing that you actually were up north like you said, except for one miscalculation on your part," Doug told me in the tone of a clever detective.

"I don't know what you mean," I continued my deception.

Seeming almost disappointed at my lack of foresight, Doug responded, "You should have turned down the speakers. I can hear the

catapults destroy the city walls because the sound's traveling through your walls and through mine." He was mad not only about the noise, but also because I had lied to him.
"How long have you been playing?" he asked.
"I don't know," I replied—truthfully, because I really did not know.
"It's noon right now." He went on, "Have you been to bed yet?"
I confessed, "Actually, I haven't. I've been up for twenty-two hours straight, and most of that time has been spent on the computer."

What is it about video games and the Internet that would lead a grown man to become consumed to this point? Video games and computers are not new inventions. The first game was introduced in 1958 at the Brookhaven National Laboratory. The game, Tennis for Two, prefigured a game that became widespread in the early 1970s, Pong. In the late 1970s, Tandy came out with the first mass-produced home computers, a development quickly followed by more complex game consoles such as Atari. Still, times have obviously changed and the role of technology in our lives has expanded greatly. In addition to incredible growth in the number of technological devices we encounter daily, the type of technology and games has also changed. While it was easy to walk away from the simplistic video games of my youth, the new games offer much more that captivate players and hold their interest. Likewise, the Internet in general and other various digital technologies are constant companions and an integral part of our modern world. The benefits of this technology are many, and yet such progress comes at a price. The number of people with a problem related to gaming and use of other devices is growing exponentially in the United States and around the world. A May 2009 study reported in *Psychological Science* found that 8.5 percent of young video gamers exhibited signs of addiction to gaming.[1] Maressa Hecht Orzack, director of the Computer Addiction Study Center at Harvard, says that her research shows that between 5 and 10 percent of Web users suffer from a Web dependency.[2] Clearly, the problem is already out of control.

Often, the reality of this problem leaves loved ones dumbfounded. Family members and friends can hardly believe it when they discover that their loved one prefers playing a game to almost every other activity, and would rather network online than spend time with people in the real world. They want to help their loved one but struggle to understand what compels someone to throw away so much. The apparent waste of time and energy shocks and even offends. Why would anyone do this? We know that alcohol, food, drugs, and gambling can overtake a person's life and become addictive. But video games and the Internet?

Indeed, the intricacies of the cyber world, and the allure of it, remain a mystery for many. Each one of the thousands of video games on the market speaks its own jargon, making it exceedingly difficult for a nongamer to achieve even a rudimentary comprehension of the particulars of a game. The Internet carries its own sort of confusion as well. Although many people use Internet networking and chat sites, the majority struggle to make sense of how an individual could stay up all night chatting with friends or customizing a MySpace page. Parents, friends, and loved ones suffer confusion because cyber junkies seem to live in a different world, which they cannot penetrate. They want to help their loved one, but they do not know how.

What are we talking about here, a bad habit or an addiction? Experts disagree on whether such a thing as cyber or gaming addiction exists. The American Psychiatric Association has been debating whether compulsive Internet use and video gaming meet the accepted criteria of addiction and whether it should be listed as a "disorder" in the next edition of its diagnostic book. I'm not a scientist and I don't claim to be an authority when it comes to alcohol or other drug problems. What I do know are the ins and outs of cyber and gaming problems and how those problems can destroy a person's life. I'm not alone in recognizing this problem. In the United States, newsgroups, community activists, government officials, teachers, and throngs of concerned parents have come together to agree that a problem exists and that solutions have been difficult to find. Other parts of the world have already accepted the existence of cyber addiction and have begun to take action. In Japan, Taiwan, Holland, China, and South Korea, the problem is widely recognized and treatment centers are well-established. South Korea considers Internet addiction a serious national health crisis and has taken an active approach toward both treating and preventing the problem.[3] In the end, then, it doesn't really matter what you call it—compulsive use, problem use or abuse, or addiction. It exhibits many similarities to other behaviors that have already been officially classified as addictive. In my mind, that's what it is, and so this book will use the terms *cyber addiction* and *gaming addiction*.

This chapter provides an overview of the cyber world. It explores who we cyber junkies are and what motivates us to spend hours and even days in front of a computer screen. In addition to discussing the drawbacks of digital technology, it describes how these technologies affect our lives in positive ways.

A New World Order

VIDEO GAMES

The world of recreation and entertainment is in the midst of a cultural shift, which purports to offer many advantages, but likewise puts many individuals in peril.

In recent years video gaming has become the primary source of entertainment for hundreds of millions of people throughout the world. According to the National Institute on Media and the Family, worldwide sales are on target to top $50 billion by 2011. Younger folks are more likely to play video games than to participate in organized sports, and studies show that the average child in the developing world spends well over forty hours per week in front of a screen. In the United States, a staggering 83 percent of children own a video game console.[4] Yet gaming is by no means a pastime only for kids. On the contrary, today's video games increasingly appeal to adults. Some studies set the average age of video gamers at a surprising thirty-three.[5]

Douglas Lowenstein, founder and former president of the Entertainment Software Association, issued a statement that captures the scope of the shift that video gaming is bringing to modern society:

> The video game industry is entering a new era where technology and creativity will fuse to produce some of the most stunning entertainment of the 21st Century. Decades from now, cultural historians will look back at this time and say it is when the definition of entertainment changed forever.[6]

I do not dispute Lowenstein's assertion, but many folks find themselves gripped by growing pains as these monumental changes in the entertainment world take root. The compelling nature of many games leads players into excess. As a society, we are only beginning to recognize that this problem exists and consequently have not figured out a way to deal with it.

Many features of video games tap into the compulsive side of human nature. I can personally attest to this. On Christmas and at other family gatherings, I often beelined for the computer or nearest video game system. In spite of my gregarious nature, some great magnetism seemed to draw me into the speechless communion I had with the cyber world. Somehow I always found a game or Web site that entranced me. I seemed to crave the multisensory stimulation. The crash, the bleeps, the constantly changing screen all melded with my psyche. In those sweet moments I was transported to a different universe.

New technologies have steadily heightened realism and allow players to feel more a part of the game, thereby increasing the potential for addiction. Excessive play impedes social and academic development. It damages relationships and, in some cases, exhibits the hallmarks of addiction. Parents, spouses, and friends of gaming addicts are searching for ways to deal with a problem that significantly disrupts addicts' lives. Few options are widely available at this point, although centers for Internet-based compulsion are beginning to crop up all over the country and around the world. Some people are forging ahead and creating their own unique pathways into recovery.

THE INTERNET, SMARTPHONES, TEXTING, AND OTHER TECHNOLOGIES

As with video games, we've seen an explosion in the development, variety, and availability of other forms of electronic devices. At last count, there were more than 4 billion cell phone users throughout the world[7] and almost 1.9 billion computer users.[8] More than 1.75 billion people regularly use the Internet. The cyber world is still experiencing exponential expansion in the number of people who make use of it and in the number of services and activities it offers.

Although not yet as ubiquitous as video games, Internet social networking sites are changing the way people connect and stay in touch. There are now thirty countries around the world that have amassed more than one million Facebook users.[9] Facebook is dominant around the world with 78 million regular users, MySpace with 67 million, Twitter with 17 million, and LinkedIn with 11 million regular users.[10] (Due to the rapidly shifting and expanding nature of social networking sites, these numbers change on a daily basis.) Industry standards define a regular user as someone who checks his or her account at least once every thirty days. These sites, along with cell phones, BlackBerrys, email, and texting, have transformed the way people stay in touch. Communication is instantaneous and constant.

Sharing ideas and artistic creation has also been facilitated. The Pew Internet and American Life Project published a study in 2009 that found that 61 percent of adults had accessed the Internet to find information related to their physical and mental health.[11] Rather than lumbering to the library to do a research project, children can access most of what they need online. Twenty-three-year-old Adam Young, an electronic music artist, had very little luck getting his music out to the public until he started using MySpace, on which his music has generated a whopping 42 million plays.[12]

While facilitating artistic exposure, communication, and networking, social networking sites can, like video games, elicit compulsive behavior. While the vast majority of users employ these sites to expand and augment their personal and professional relationships, some use them at the expense of real-time human contact. Likewise, many use Internet chat engines to keep up with cyber friends to the detriment of one-on-one human interaction.

Just as social networking allows people the sense of being plugged-in, smartphones (Internet-capable with games), PDAs (personal digital assistants, which have mostly been superseded by smartphones), texting, and compulsive email checking provide the potential to stay connected with the Internet and other people without interruption. None of these technologies are bad, and can actually be quite useful in business and relationships, but they easily lend themselves to compulsion. There is the "reward" and social satisfaction of getting a text or an email. People look forward to it, and to some extent, it can make them feel important and connected. For people who are more vulnerable to addiction, the slight psychological boost that most of us feel when we get a friendly text or email may instead be intensive and can become all-encompassing, causing them to neglect or not fully engage with responsibilities and important people in their lives. When a compulsive email checker with a smartphone is in a business meeting, for example, he or she is probably not paying full attention to the information being conveyed because the urge to check email yet again is irresistible. When a text-adept teen has a phone in school, he or she can become so skilled at concealment and "blind" texting that this activity can go on throughout the whole school day, constantly distracting and ensuring academic underperformance or even failure. Many students with ADHD who attend my ADHD study groups compulsively send text messages; some students send over one hundred a day.

Surfing the Internet can itself become excessive and compulsive. Some folks find great joy in discovering new information, especially the unusual and arcane. A nineteen-year-old who I coached came to me because he was spending six to eight hours a day searching for unusual videos. He had dozens of sites he would search, and when he happened upon a video he particularly enjoyed, he would email the link to friends and family, most of whom, he later learned, never watched these videos. The search for these videos was so engaging to him that it swallowed up his life.

Most of us use the Internet and our cell phones to stay in touch and find useful information from time to time, but cyber addicts become consumed by these technologies and end up not being able to use them responsibly or in moderation.

A Sedentary Lifestyle

Video games, like television, often function as a babysitter because of their capacity to capture attention over long periods. Many parents accept video games as a way to keep their children out of trouble. Children congregate around a game console much more often than they do in parks or vacant lots. They do not venture outdoors for pickup basketball, street hockey, or touch football because they can play these and other games in the virtual world. As a result, physical activity among children has declined.

The massive popularity of video gaming and the Internet exacerbates the disturbing sedentary trend among American youth and consequent rise in obesity. With parents working longer hours and two-income families the norm, parents are not around as much to ensure healthy choices. In my professional experience with young people, excessive gaming, in-school texting and Internet use, and obsessive social network use often accompany poor performance in school. Many children choose video gaming and their Internet pursuits over physical activity, chores and other responsibilities, homework, or friends.

Why We Play—the Allure

In South Korea, Taiwan, Japan, and now even the United States, video game adepts attain celebrity status. They prepare for competitions like athletes train for the Olympics. Always searching for an edge over their opponents, they strive to perfect their grips on their controllers and fine-tune hand and arm posture. They choose one game and devote their lives to mastering it. These world-class gamers can look forward to prizes ranging from $10,000 to upwards of $250,000. They appear in magazines and on radio and TV interviews, and they are seen as role models. They game for greed, glory, and fame. The rest of us, however, game and use the Internet for reasons that are not so cut-and-dried.

No one model encompasses the wide array of reasons that we are consumed by our games or other digital technologies. Through working on myself and with other addicted video gamers and cyber junkies, I have discovered some common threads that link us together. Most gamers and cyber users I have encountered exhibit a combination of motivations, some of which, of course, overlap. There is nothing inherently unhealthy or wrong with any of these until the person's behavior tips toward addiction. When cyber activity becomes a substitute for material and relationship success, it also is becoming a potent means of evading what the individual sees as unpleasant realities.

FINDING COMMUNITY IN THE GLOBAL VILLAGE

The lack of community stands as one of the great sicknesses of the modern world. When I was growing up in the 1970s and early 1980s, people knew their neighbors. If one mother needed to run out to the store, her kids would simply go over to someone else's house until their mother returned. People would borrow an egg or a cup of sugar when they were making a cake. Most parents don't bake cakes anymore, and running out of a specific ingredient certainly means a trip to the store rather than a short walk to the next-door neighbor. We have become more self-sufficient, but also more separate.

Cyber junkies have developed our own remedies for this sad state of human interaction. On a daily basis, we chat with people in our cyber communities. We join gaming clans that have members in Taiwan, India, Europe, Africa, and Australia. We become cyber friends with people from all over the globe. A friend of mine was a member of a Counter-Strike clan. A clan is a team of gamers who typically meet online at the same time every night to play together and challenge other clans. Some clans spend more than twenty hours a week "together," making the contact time much more intensive than most real-time relationships. Although most of the people in these social relationships never meet in person, this is not always the case. My friend's clan planned trips together all over the world, and although many of them had previously lacked social skills, somehow the game brought them together and allowed them to form tight bonds. This friend even took Spanish classes so he could communicate with a clan member from Spain. For him, the game was a source of inspiration.

Certainly this anecdote paints a rosy picture, but it demonstrates the communal and international nature of the cyber world. The absence of community in modern society motivates some of us to seek it online. For many, our cyber relations represent the first time that we have genuinely felt part of a group. Without some significant substitute, we will not easily relinquish these hard-earned connections.

Not only do online multiplayer games and social networking sites help us find a sense of community, but forming such relationships in the virtual world eliminates most of the effort required to create and maintain social networks. Gamers come home, log on to the computer, and have multiple messages waiting for them from their online buddies. They discuss strategy, and even support each other through life's many difficulties. Some cyber users turn away from family and real-world friends to indulge online relationships, while others with poor social skills avail themselves of anonymous connections so that they do not feel isolated and alone. Obviously, there is nothing wrong with having online friends, but many cyber-addicted folks become far too dependent on connections with people they have never actually met. Their social skills stagnate.

ACHIEVEMENT

Video games provide many possibilities for success and triumph. Many who are drawn most strongly to gaming are those who lack other opportunities for achievement. We seek power and status from our games. We hunger for advancement through the different ages and levels. We want to progress with lightning speed. Our goal is beating the game as quickly as possible. For some people, creating a huge Facebook friend list can be seen as an achievement, while some MySpace users obsess on the achievement of having the "coolest" profile.

Gamers tend to be hypercompetitive, constantly on the lookout for a forum to prove ourselves. In my childhood years, exercising this competitive urge required foraging through the neighborhood to round up enough kids to play touch football, street hockey, or baseball. But now, millions of playmates are available simply by logging on to the computer. Players can now be "rounded up" from the entire world! For hours every night, competitive gamers test their skills repeatedly.

We often measure our self-worth against our performance in a certain game. One young man, Jay, came to see me in my capacity as an ADHD life coach. This troubled nineteen-year-old had extraordinarily low self-esteem. "I will never be what my parents want me to be," he tearfully admitted during one of our sessions. "They think I'm going to become a doctor, but I've flunked calculus three times," he said. Jay had failed to live up to just about every expectation his parents had for him. He considered himself a complete failure. His face would light up, however, when he recounted his streak of victories in Super Smash Bros. and Mario Kart, two Nintendo 64 games he had completely mastered. I, too, am good at those old school games, and on several occasions, we played together—a technique I use to break the ice and create a bond. As we played, an arrogant and trash-talking young man emerged.

I only beat him once, but this event unsettled him. "You only beat me because I'm having a bad day," he snapped. "I'll come back tomorrow and show you how it's done." We never played after that. His fragile self-esteem would not let him risk losing to me again. Video games gave him perhaps the only success he had ever had. He was a "somebody" in those games and had no intention of giving up that hard-earned status.

For players such as Jay, winning is the very definition of success. Other gamers measure accomplishment by accumulating the in-game symbols of wealth and rank, like gold, top-tier armor, or magic spells. They maintain interest in a game as long as the possibility for increasing status continues. In-game money is made by defeating monsters, mining and farming, or buying and selling goods. Players use the money to purchase upgrades and items that will be useful in later quests.

Some players short-circuit the arduous process of progression in the game by purchasing a game's currency online with real-world money and using it to inflate their character's power, status, or experience level. Several in-game currencies trade on eBay against the United States dollar. In the Far East, cyber entrepreneurs have established a sort of video game "sweat shop," in which gamer-workers sit at computers and perform repetitive tasks in certain online games to amass virtual currency. This money is traded for real money online. Thus, players may buy their way to the top.

ESCAPE

The endless possibilities for achievement in today's video games allow gamers to escape the sad lack of success or meaningful relationships in their lives. "I come home from work, plug in my PlayStation, and killing the bad guys lets me let go of the frustrations of the day," said one participant at my cyber addiction group as he began his weekly personal inventory, which we call a check-in. "The trouble is that I can't stop playing once I start."

Online social networkers and Internet junkies can also be motivated by escape. Many who lack social skills and contacts throw themselves into the cyber world, amassing "friends" while they have little contact with real humans. But social networking and the Internet provide some comfort and soothing. This comes at a price, however, because their focus on the Internet is an escape from dealing with the issues that prevent them from having the kinds of social lives they would really like to have.

For example, the man mentioned previously was able to release his stress through his PlayStation gaming, but he already had a troubled marriage and he stayed on his game instead of interacting with his wife. He found her to be very demanding. He told the group that she constantly needled him about doing household chores, making more money, and going to church. From his perspective, complying with one of his wife's requests only led to a host of others. Instead of counseling, he chose the cyber-male-bonding experience of Brothers in Arms: Earned in Blood, a World War II squad-level simulation game. As he fought in the crumbling ruins of Bastogne to keep the Nazis at bay, his marriage crumbled. He escaped into a new reality instead of combating the difficulties in his own.

To some extent, all the gamers I see at my groups and in my coaching practice have issues in their lives that the cyber world helps them avoid. These issues are not the result of their excessive cyber activities, but rather are the factors that drive them to those activities in the first place. Many of these people never developed problem-solving skills. Others simply prefer a make-believe world.

MY STORY: STUCK IN A WORLD OF FANTASY

As a boy, I was usually bored out of my mind while sitting in school. I spent most of my time in a world of fantasy and imagination. Most of my flights of imagination revolved around being a military hero who saved the innocent or liberated the oppressed. Taking over the school was the theme of my self-aggrandizing daydreams. I played many characters. They interacted with each other in my mind; my thoughts switching from one persona to another.

continues

"Joe, how are we going to get through Sister Carol's defense perimeter?" one of the commander's underlings asked. "We're going to have helicopters drop us on the roof," Joe answered confidently, "and then we're going to break through the skylights. They'll be forced to take notice of us and meet our demands for longer recess and less homework." I had conversations like these in my mind all day long. I believe this tendency underlies my strong attachment to video game playing. I believe video games represent for me, as for many, an attempt to escape from the dullness of everyday reality.

ROLE PLAYING

Most game enthusiasts thrive on fantasy. They increasingly identify with the characters they create and mold. Their online persona often possesses attributes that they wish they had in real life. An introvert lacking social skills allows him- or herself to be gregarious with a large group of in-game acquaintances. A physically weak individual controls a strong and powerful character. People who feel that their lives lack meaning perform with purpose in the game, defeating the wicked to protect the innocent. Fantasy is the addictive juice for role-playing-oriented individuals. They are driven by the opportunities to become someone else, to exist in a different time, or to live lives filled with meaning.

Role players often possess infinite patience, because acquiring interesting and advanced character attributes entails mind-numbing repetition. One may have to wander around one level and kill the same monster in the same way three hundred times to get enough experience to move up a level or enter a new maze. They gladly suffer the tedium because of the deep satisfaction the game gives them. "Instead of just watching a movie," one rather philosophical role player told me, "I'm in it! What could be more exciting than that?"

Role players not only derive excitement from their games, they come to rely on them for social interaction.

Role playing, however, is not only a component in video games, but also in social networking. In social networking, users craft their profiles to project the image they want, and perhaps to which they aspire. Such an image may be very different than who they really are. Since much communication in social networking takes place not face-to-face but through technology (Internet, online chatting, texting), this image can be maintained until such time as an in-person meeting is arranged. Role playing is also often used during Internet dating. People use outdated pictures and lie about everything from weight and age to occupation and marital status. When it comes to Internet communication, deception is easy.

CONTROL

One of the ironies is that many cyber junkies who make their way to me and my support groups are the products of strict, albeit well-meaning, parents. "We really regulated computer and video game use when he was growing up," a sixteen-year-old video game addict's father earnestly told me. "And then around the age of thirteen, he started staying in his room by himself all the time, glued to RuneScape," the boy's father said, as he struggled to understand where he and his wife had "gone wrong." Many teenagers evade excessive parental control by losing themselves in the alternate reality that video games provide. When we find a situation to be hopeless or beyond our powers to influence, we dissociate from that situation. We shut ourselves off from others in order to exist in a world where we have complete autonomy.

The cyber world is often a refuge for those whose lives have gone off track. Kyle's parents came to see me after their bright and athletic son had slipped into depression. "He used to be so vivacious and involved," his mother told me during a meeting I had with the whole family. "Now, his whole life centers on that game." Kyle once participated in high school musicals, often landing the starring role because of his incredible voice. He played sports and was active in his family's church.

Kyle went off to college, and shortly thereafter an illness prevented him from playing sports. He determined around the same time that he was never going to be a professional singer, so he gave up the theater. Stripped of the two loves of his life, he fell into depression and started playing an online game called A Tale in the Desert. In this game, set in ancient Egypt, players cooperate to build a civilization from scratch.

"The game made me feel like I was doing something, and I didn't know what else to do," Kyle told me. His former life in shambles, the game gave him a sense of power and purpose. As we discussed the situation, it became clear that Kyle wanted the same sense of flow and excitement that he had had in high school, but felt unable to forge a new chapter in his life. This lack of control lay beneath his addictive gaming binges. His healing process involved taking control of his life once again.

OUTLET FOR AGGRESSION

Many people maintain that video games produce violence. I believe, in contrast, that video games simply provide an outlet, albeit a sometimes unhealthy one, for preexisting aggressive tendencies. Many video games bring out traits that might otherwise lie dormant. I have witnessed, for example, seemingly calm teens turn irate and nasty while playing online shooting games such as Call of Duty. They talk trash, insulting their opponents (from the safety of their headsets) and attempting to incite them to anger. They hope that these tactics will throw opponents off balance and give them an edge. I know of several teens who enjoy the opportunities to talk trash more than they like playing the game itself. "It's the only way I can get my anger out," eighteen-year-old Victor told me. "I feel better after I play."

Some players engage in a disturbing practice called teabagging. When killing an opponent's on-screen character, they have their own character kneel down on top of the other character before the body disappears from the screen in a move designed to show dominance and, of course, to humiliate. I have found several Web forum listings that offer advice on how best to perform this maneuver.

One fourteen-year-old, Tyler, admitted to me that he engaged in this practice. "I never had a way to get my anger out before," he told me. "People make me so angry sometimes, but I never say anything. The game lets me get it out without actually hurting anyone." I eventually learned that Tyler felt socially isolated and had been picked on a great deal in grade school. Video games did not produce his anger but rather gave him a way to express it.

Many of the young people who come to my groups—especially the males—have anger management issues alongside their excessive video gaming habits. Parents tell me stories of bashed-in walls, broken windows, and screaming episodes that occurred after a particularly poor performance in a video game. Although many parents blame video games for their child's anger, I firmly believe that the anger existed long before they found a game that allowed them to focus and release it. Certain games give gamers an outlet for their anger, but unfortunately, most never develop the ability to express it in a healthy way. I have referred dozens of clients to therapists for anger management.

While those who excessively use social networking sites and the Internet do not, in my experience, suffer as a group from excessive anger issues, they do generally suffer from emotional avoidance. The obsessive behavior is done, in many cases, to avoid dealing with unpleasant emotional realities.

DISCOVERY

Chris does not care if he wins, loses, or draws. Satisfaction for this man comes from finding new twists to a game or uncovering a glitch that no one has yet discovered. Chris is the consummate observer and delights in discovering new sources of stimuli. As an example, he got fulfillment in the game Legend of Zelda, where he found that playing a flute in front of a certain stone in the game caused a fairy to appear who could heal his character. His find left him elated for a week.

Discovery-oriented gamers are engaged by novelty. They pursue every nook and cranny of the game to tease out any possibility of something new. This type of individual attains a certain achievement from having completed every possible permutation of the game. A discovery-oriented gamer is less concerned with quick completion of a game, but obsessed with attaining certainty that he or she has performed every possible task, quest, and challenge the game has to offer.

Chris, for example, does not rush through a game, but rather savors every opportunity to learn something new. A daydreamer in school, Chris spent little or no time on his homework, but was absorbed by Legend of Zelda for up to eight hours daily. His exploits became so well known in his neighborhood and at school that neighbor children and schoolmates used to drop by his house simply to watch him play. He visited realms in the games the other kids did not even know existed. He had hopes of becoming a professional gamer.

When tested by a psychologist, Chris's full-scale IQ was found to be 135, clearly in the gifted range. Unfortunately, his superior intelligence and penchant for discovery have not translated into success in real life. At the age of twenty-five, Chris lives at his mother's house and works at a movie theater. He is working with me on a plan to achieve some of the long-held aspirations that excessive gaming has prevented him from attaining.

For people such as Chris, video gaming is a substitute. Chris wants to feel fully alive, but he doesn't take the steps to make that happen. The fulfillment that he derives from games is actually an approximation of what he wants out of life. This fact can be applied to all addicted gamers. Our individual motivations for gaming may differ, but the root of why we game is the same. We seek games that give us some semblance of what we do not have in our real lives. Finding the right game for each individual's addictive profile gets easier and easier every year as the number of new games increases exponentially.

Like many video gaming addicts, Chris also spends a lot of time discovering "neat" things on the Internet. He is motivated by the possibility of finding unusual Web sites, videos, and "little-known" information. Discovery is also a key element for many who obsessively surf the Internet.

Who We Are

It's important to understand the types of individuals who are drawn to cyber activities. I ask you to suspend for a short time the effects of what the cyber world has done to your life or to your loved one. Step into our world for a brief time, and walk with us in our shoes. Cyber addictions are phenomena best understood from the inside.

WIZARDS OUT OF WATER

"The universe is full of magical things, patiently waiting for our wits to grow sharper."
—Eden Phillpotts

Many people write off cyber junkies as unproductive losers and perhaps even brand us as stupid. Quite the contrary, we are creative and imaginative souls. However, we fail to uncover a way to productively channel our gifts and form the human connections we crave. We dream of dynamic, purposeful, contact-filled, and exciting lives, but we just do not put together the steps needed to fulfill our vision. Movies such as *Star Wars*, *Lord of the Rings*, and *Harry Potter* strike a chord deep within us because we long for magic, an infusion of energy and focus that would allow us to actualize the brilliance we are certain we carry within.

Over years of working with cyber addicts, I have come to the conclusion that could-be future Nobel laureates are right now planted in chairs expending all of their intellectual and emotional resources into fruitless screen time. If you could peer into our minds, you would discover them bubbling over with insights and ideas. Find someone addicted to the cyber world, and you will often discover a person of superior intelligence. Many gaming addicts I have encountered have a genius-level IQ. When this intelligent person was a student, you probably would have described him or her as an underachiever and perhaps peppered him or her with subtle but frequent shaming: "You're so smart. I can't believe you're not getting all As in school." You might have provided a litany of career choices you considered appropriate for someone with so much potential: "You should become a doctor, lawyer, or maybe even a nuclear physicist."

Many of us, though, end up working menial jobs just to pay the bills so we can maximize cyber time and feel that connected surge within ourselves and the profound bond we experience with other players and "friends" from all over the world. Many of the adults among us are actually gainfully employed, only to come home to ignore our families, because to us they are annoying distractions. We shrink from career or relationship opportunities, but in the game we are smack dab in the middle of an international community, relating and connecting to others. We feel part of something larger than ourselves.

AN ALTERNATE REALITY

We are willing to go in any direction that takes us away from the dreariness of reality. For those of us who overindulge in online networking and communication such as email and texting, our real-world relationships leave us unsatisfied, so we prefer the ones we cultivate in cyberland. Since most of our online friends live far away, there is little chance that we will meet them and thus ruin the fantasy.

This alternate reality is most poignant when it comes to video games. Video games supply players with a parallel universe that allows us to indulge fantasies, fly off on imaginative tangents, and exercise supreme control over other worlds. We hunger for the feeling of being fully alive that eludes us in reality. When we are in the "game zone," however, we enthusiastically enter a different dimension.

Time stands still for us as the challenges of the game inspire us to bring forth our arsenal of exceptional abilities. With super-human perception, we identify the minutest of changes on our map board or gaming screen. We are capable of nonstop play for ten, fifteen, even twenty-four hours at a time. Although we have trouble organizing our bedrooms and closets or keeping track of important papers, we successfully manage entire economic systems in our games. We exercise steadfast patience as we lie in wait for our virtual adversaries to stumble into our clutches. We doggedly pursue the next reward or level in our games, sometimes taking months to achieve our goal. We gloss over many crucial details in our real lives, yet exhibit laser-like concentration on our electronic battlegrounds. We are the stars, the geniuses, the saviors of our cyber universe.

ASPERGER'S, ADHD, AND OTHER COMORBIDITIES

A high percentage of the folks I work with possess artistic and creative powers. They waste them, of course, sitting in front of a computer screen or television. An equally high percentage have either Asperger's syndrome (AS) or attention-deficit/hyperactivity disorder (ADHD). I have found that both of these conditions seem to lend themselves to excessive video gaming.

When an addicted video gamer comes to one of my groups, 90 percent of the time there is a *comorbidity*, a fancy term meaning that two or more conditions exist in the same person. I have had a number of young people with AS, ADHD, bipolar disorder, and clinical depression attend my support groups.

Asperger's syndrome, a high-functioning form of autism, is generally characterized by difficulties in social interaction as well as by restricted or limited areas of interest. Individuals with AS often have troubles in school similar to those with ADHD: organizing, maintaining focus, and long-term planning. The singular interest of many Asperger's kids I see is video games. I see them in action because we take video game breaks during my study groups.

Young people with AS experience a significantly greater intensity when playing video games than any other individuals I have seen. When they play, they often breathe heavily. They gyrate in their seats and make jerky movements with their legs and arms when they get to crucial parts of the game. Their intensity while playing is often enough to unnerve other kids. They seem literally to merge with the game.

Given that AS folks usually struggle with social interaction, obsession with games is particularly troubling. One bright spot in this situation, however, is that if we can enter into their video game world, we have an opportunity to connect with them in a deep way.

An exciting study recently emerged from the annual meeting of the British Psychological Association. According to Dr. John Charlton of the University of Bolton in England and Ian Danforth of Whitman College in Washington State, "Gamers who appear to be addicted to playing computer/video games show some of the same negative personality traits as people with Asperger's syndrome."[13] The main traits seen were neuroticism, and lack of extraversion and agreeableness. The researchers believe that these people do not have Asperger's syndrome but exhibit some of the same characteristics because they find it easier to empathize with computer systems than other people.

Attention-deficit/hyperactivity disorder is a condition usually characterized by difficulty in a few key areas, such as maintaining concentration over long periods, planning, organizing, and completing tasks. Since these areas are all important for academic performance, those with ADHD often struggle in school. In my role as an ADHD coach, I help these individuals develop programs for success in school and their careers.

Given that approximately one-third of individuals with ADHD will eventually have a problem with substance abuse, it should come as no surprise that many of the people with ADHD whom I work with also suffer from video gaming addiction.[14] Those with

ADHD have great difficulty with repetition and routine. Without going into a lot of neurological details, the baseline of activity in the ADHD brain is lower for routine and repetition. What is often termed distractibility comes from the fact that a person with ADHD quickly gets bored with stimuli and seeks new sources of stimulation. Edward Hallowell, in his book *Driven to Distraction*, explains how individuals with ADHD get distracted because they need to constantly seek new stimulation to keep their brains active.[15] Video games provide a reliable source of constantly changing stimuli. Those with ADHD often become reliant on them.

Interestingly, I have been gathering data on how medication for ADHD impacts excessive cyber behaviors. Although more formal research is needed in this area, my initial findings through conversations and interviews with more than fifty students over the past four years strongly suggest that medication reduces excessive and compulsive cyber use among those with ADHD. One sixteen-year-old student of mine said, "When I take my meds, my hand-eye coordination is not as fast, so I don't enjoy playing as much. Like when I play Blitz 2000, I get sacked a lot more when I'm on Adderall. I also don't have the urge to play as much when I am on my meds."

Bipolar disorder is a serious condition marked by highs and lows of mood, and serious swings in one direction or the other can be accompanied by hallucinations, delusions, sleep disturbances, psychosis, and extremely erratic behavior. Experts worry that the symptoms of bipolar disorder can be exacerbated by excessive video game play. I have had no less than a dozen clients come to me for excessive video gaming who later were diagnosed with bipolar disorder.

Potential Benefits of Cyber Technology

The cyber world offers many positive aspects. I believe we need to learn to live with today's technology, not banish it. Contrary to much of the recent negative press, video games, social networking, and other cyber activities offer many advantages.

VIDEO GAMES

"What we've found is that success as a business leader
may depend on skills as a gamer."
—Jim Spohrer, IBM research director

The world seems to be changing in favor of those who love video games. Our game skills correlate to heightened abilities in many fields. In a 2004 study of surgeons, for example, those who played video games for more than three hours a week were 37 percent less likely to make mistakes during a specific operation and finished the procedure 27 percent faster.[16] This is no wonder, since many surgical techniques rely on a video interface to guide the surgeon's hands. Laparoscopic surgery, for example, involves using a small camera and devices controlled by joysticks. Obviously, video game play enhances hand-eye coordination as well as visual precision and perception. Electronic battlefield monitoring makes video gamers ideal soldiers or sailors. Recruiting officers around the country have realized this fact for a decade, and the U.S. Army has designed its own video game to teach soldiers and prospective soldiers valuable military skills. Air Force predator drones are controlled from bunkers by operators using technology that looks and feels very much like a video game. As more jobs and tasks involve the worker interfacing with a screen, video game adepts will enjoy greater appreciation of their abilities.

Educational researchers tout the benefits of simulation and role-playing games because of the vocabulary, reasoning, and social skills they boost.[17] Many teachers across the country now use educational video games in their classrooms as an interactive way to convey information. They have recognized the potential of this medium to more fully engage students in the learning process.[18]

Additionally, oncologists have tapped into the power of video games to get their young patients more involved in curing their disease. The game Re-Mission was developed specifically for young cancer patients. It is the first video game scientifically proven to improve therapeutic adherence and treatment success for young people with cancer.[19] Young people who played this game maintained higher blood levels of chemotherapy drugs versus the control group, as well as higher rates of adherence to cancer treatment regimens. Many studies show benefits for video games for elderly folks in maintaining physical and mental agility, as well as the potential for online social networking to help them keep in touch with friends and family and even make new friends. Possibilities for positive applications seem endless.

Most excessive gamers, however, fail to develop a positive and balanced relationship to games. Some of us temporarily stop gaming, but to keep from returning to games, we must find an adventure in the real world that is worthy of our skills. Luckily, the business environment is in the midst of change, and it may be that the world is starting to realize that it needs many of our abilities.

America's business leaders are beginning to take notice of the leadership potential of many online gamers. Millions of gamers play daily and compete in multifaceted virtual surroundings. These players organize, build skills, and function in many different roles. Leaders come forward who are competent in "recruiting, organizing, motivating, and directing large groups of players toward a common goal." They develop the ability to make decisions quickly, with imperfect information.[20] These individuals regularly take calculated risks based on information supplied by their team. Some corporations, seeking to develop more effective managers, already have virtual training modules designed to exploit these facets of online gaming. Geneva Trading, a stock and commodities firm in Chicago, uses video game simulations to assess potential recruits. Company president Mary McDonnell said, "It is unlikely that we would hire someone who didn't show good proficiency at a Game Boy or online poker or similar videotype game where hand-to-eye coordination is important."

Corporate environments also demand that managers skillfully diffuse conflict, as well as create an atmosphere of bold openness. Although excessive gamers often struggle socially, through online games they do develop these capacities as a matter of course:

In online games, perhaps because players are represented as avatars and are not face-to-face with each other, heated disagreements are common and accepted. Players even claim to become desensitized to group conflict over time. Perhaps this kind of passionate honesty has a place of value in the modern enterprise as well.[21]

This conclusion was reached by an intense study performed by none other than IBM, an icon of American business. Those who excel at video games have useful skills to offer the world. My work with addicted video gamers centers on helping them apply these skills in productive ways.

ONLINE SOCIAL NETWORKING

Most people use social networking sites, texting, and online chatting (Yahoo!, MSN, and AOL instant messengers) simply to keep in touch with close friends. Families with loved ones fighting in Iraq or Afghanistan no longer have to wait for days or weeks to hear from them. Soldiers in the field often update their Facebook, MySpace, or Twitter accounts on a daily basis. This certainly makes it easier to bear the burden of long-term separation.

These tools make it easier to maintain and expand one's group of friends and contacts. Studies suggest that people with high self-esteem use these sites to communicate more effectively with their peer group, while those with lower self-esteem often use them to try to make their way into new social groups.[22] Many succeed in achieving social compensation through social networking sites.

Emerging adults are using social networking sites to maintain large, diffuse networks of friends, with a positive impact on their accumulation of bridging social capital. Although it is tempting to consider these large networks of acquaintances as shallow, in reality these connections have true potential for generating benefits for users. Moreover, online social network services appear to offer important [relationship-building potential], especially for those who otherwise face difficulties in forming and maintaining the large and heterogeneous networks of contacts that are sources of social capital.[23]

People with no trouble making friends and those with social difficulties both use social networking sites to enhance their interpersonal connections. Nonprofit organizations use them to build their fundraising and volunteer networks, while politicians build electoral and donor followings through these media. Business people offer their services and find appropriate consultation through sites such as LinkedIn. University freshmen employ social networking sites in the weeks and months into their first term to find like-minded individuals with similar interests and values. Social networking sites offer almost limitless potential for bringing and keeping people together as well as enhancing preexisting relationships. For better or worse, they are revolutionizing human interaction.

The Next Step

Digital technology is here to stay, and its potential to transform many parts of our lives in positive ways is immense. Cyber obsessions, on the other hand, drain the world of vast reserves of talent. Our country currently lacks the understanding that would allow it to help the cyber-oriented individual take his or her rightful place as a responsible, respectable, and contributing member of society. Our goal must be not to simply get these folks to stop their excessive behavior, but rather to assist them in channeling their enormous potential into exciting and worthwhile pursuits.

In the next chapter, we go behind the scenes to learn more about the world that cyber junkies find so compelling.

CHAPTER 2

choose your poison

> "Why is it drug addicts and computer
> aficionados are both called users?"
> **Clifford Stoll, astronomer and writer**

The title for this chapter includes the word *poison*, which is a reference to the fact that while the massive diversity of electronic devices carries many benefits, for some these devices become toxins that invade people's lives and prevent them from growing, developing, and being happy. This chapter takes you through some of the ways that the cyber world becomes poisonous as well as discusses the reasons that predispose some individuals to this toxin.

Social Networking Basics

SOCIAL NETWORKING SITES

Social networking sites are generally offered free to users and generate income from advertising. They typically consist of a profile that contains personal information about the individual as well as a list of his or her extended network of friends on the system. High-tech sites such as Facebook also have a host of applications that users may use to develop their profiles. Many of these enhancements are zany and fun. On my Facebook profile, for example, I used an application entitled, "Which Theologian Are You?" I answered a series of questions which then determined that I was most like Menno Simons, the founder of the Mennonites. So his picture now figures on my Facebook profile.

I find this quite amusing. Other such profile-enhancing applications include things such as "Which Star Wars Character Are
You?" and "Which '80s Band Are You?" as well as the possibility
of joining social action groups related to an array of causes like
environmentalism, politics, and helping the less fortunate. Social
networking sites combine networking, fun, and social action and
even provide a platform many folks use to invite friends to con-
certs, parties, and a variety of other events.

Twitter is akin to text messaging, but you can do it over the
Web and reach not just one person, but perhaps thousands. For
most of us, especially those who are not technology-savvy, the
value of Twitter is not as easily appreciated as that of Facebook.
Messages you send are called "tweets." Users get more immediate responses with Twitter, and "it seems to live somewhere
between the worlds of email, instant messaging and blogging.
Twitter encourages constant 'linking out' to anywhere and, in
that respect, is more analogous to a pure search engine, another
way to find people and content all over the Net."[1] Twitter users
thrive on the ability to pose a question and get a rapid response,
and many crave being able to tap into the collective consciousness of people in their network.[2] Twitter marches to the fast-
paced beat of technology and appeals to people who might be
described as "on the move."

MySpace gained popularity quickly among bands, who appreciated the ease with which one could create a profile, display
photos, convey information about upcoming performances, and
share music. Because of its strong association with musicians and
bands, the site possessed a certain avant-garde quality. Users felt
that the site allowed them to plug in to pop culture and to the local
music and artistic scenes. While MySpace's popularity has taken
a hit due to Facebook's wide appeal, many users are still drawn to
the free graphics and layout options that allow pretty much anyone and everyone to create a personalized profile, a cyber reflection of who they are, or at least of who they want others to think
they are. Like Facebook, MySpace also allows users to form groups
of like-minded individuals and stay in touch with them.

Friendster provides services and opportunities similar to those offered by Facebook and MySpace, but this social networking site is primarily an Asian networking phenomenon and accounts for the majority of social networking hits in Asian countries. LinkedIn, on the other hand, is specific to business people who want to network with people who might need their services or find someone to service their commercial needs. LinkedIn profiles focus on an individual's business experience, projects, education, and training.

The fundamental principle that links all social networking sites is simply to forge and maintain connections. They can do this very well but also present cyber-oriented folks with a new set of challenges.

SOCIAL NETWORKING AND SCHOOL

The Internet has become a social haven, especially for teens. Social networking computer sites can become an addiction in and of themselves. Teens and young adults sit at the computer, ostensibly to do their homework, and have MySpace, AOL Instant Messenger, and Facebook running simultaneously. If a message or comment comes in, they respond quickly and may be distracted for long periods of time. They may augment their Internet networking with the occasional cell phone text message. They spend hours personalizing and editing their MySpace and Facebook pages. Their school work gets done slowly, incompletely, or not at all.

For these folks, being plugged into such a vast social network is incredibly satisfying. The impulse to stay "connected" is irresistible. I have seen many compulsive gamers beat their addiction only to succumb to the allure of computer-aided social networking.

For those addicted to online multiplayer games (discussed later), the most satisfying aspects of the game are often the social ones. They belong to guilds and clans and actively participate in gaming forums and message boards. Many who give up their games are not willing to relinquish online social networking and go on to become Facebook, MySpace, and AOL Instant Messenger addicts.

While online social networking, chatting, and surfing the Web serve useful functions for most who utilize them, some users have hidden motivations that lead them into compulsion. The Internet often becomes a diversion that distracts people from the hard-to-bear realities of their lives. Rather than enhancing their life situation, it consumes them.

ONLINE CHATTING, TEXTING, SMARTPHONES, AND EMAIL

Online chatting involves logging on to a chat system, which activates a window. You can see in this window who among your friends is also logged in and communicate with them in real time. The most common of these systems are AOL Instant Messenger, Yahoo! Messenger, and Windows Live Messenger (formerly MSN Messenger), but the social networking sites, as well as the Gmail system, also offer real-time chat. For most, this communication method is an easy and cost-free way to keep in touch with friends all over the world. As I can personally attest, chatting can also become obsessive. After I gave up video games, I often chatted with friends until five or six in the morning. It was not about staying in touch, but rather was the engaging rush of having eight, ten, maybe twenty chats going simultaneously. It ceased to become a means to communicate for me and turned into an unhealthy and destructive behavior, due mostly to lack of sleep. Chatting can also be a way for people with social issues to avoid real-time human contact.

Compulsive email checking, texting, and using smartphones can be used easily in a way that, like online chatting, allows folks to avoid facing their deficits in social skills. Research is needed to determine the extent that relying on email, texting, and online communication is handicapping the interpersonal skills of the present generation of children, teens, and young adults, who are increasingly relying on these forms of communication. One of the most important benchmarks for assessing whether cyber activities rise to the level of addiction is whether they enhance one's life or impair it. Impairment, in this sense, refers to damage to friendships, family ties, career, and other activities from which the person once derived pleasure and satisfaction.

Video Games

THE EQUIPMENT

Video gaming encompasses an incredible array of possibilities. Many still use a video game console, which is a self-contained device that hooks up to the television. Some games consoles, such as the Xbox 360, can also be easily hooked into the Internet. Plugging into the Internet allows players to go to a special Web site where they can connect with other players from all over the world. So rather than being limited to playing against the computer or a few people in the same room, hundreds of thousands or even millions of other players around the world are potential opponents. Such online interactive options are available with many computer games as well. With a computer game, you load the program onto the computer and, thus, if the game allows for online multiplayer matches, it is easy to access it through the Internet. Games can also be played on iPods, and many cell phones now come equipped with Internet access.

THE GAMES

All games are not created equal. Some carry greater risk for addiction than others. From my professional experience, I have developed a rating scale that ranges from one to ten: the higher the number, the higher the potential for a game to become addictive. This scale takes into account the capacity of a game to captivate attention for multiple hours in one sitting as well as its ability to sustain interest over longer periods of time (weeks, months, or even years). In addition, my rating scale evaluates the extent to which a game contains enough reward potential to induce players into ever-increasing amounts of game time.

Games with a rating of one to three carry low potential for excessive or addictive play. Few individuals become addicted to the low-tech and repetitive games in this rating band, although it can happen. Games with ratings between four and six can become addictive, but are less likely to lead to long-term (more than three months) addictive play. Games in this rating band are more likely to lead to short-term excessive play that peters out after players tire of the game. Games rated seven to ten possess elements that easily lead to addictive play, especially in those predisposed to addiction. These games contain a virtually endless supply of rewards to keep players interested. Players may also get hooked socially, because most players of games in this rating band join online clans and guilds, which can quickly become a primary social outlet.

The Lightweights of the Gaming World

From my professional and personal experience, lightweight games carry a low to medium risk for addiction. Many people play these games without any hint of excess. Most use the games in these categories to simply pass the time, but some players still become addicted. These lightweight games fall into the lower rating bands in my rating scale.

Puzzle Games

Puzzle games deal with logic, language, trivia, mindless repetition, and visual-spatial skills. They have no themes or characters. Text Twist, a Yahoo! game, consists of an interminable set of timed trials that involve making words out of a group of six alternating letters—sort of an intense version of Scrabble. I know several teens who turn to Text Twist for hours when they should be working on a project for school.

Tetris, a very popular puzzle game, can be played on cell phones, and I know kids who play the game in class instead of paying attention to the teacher. Tetris belongs to the visual-spatial category and involves different colored shapes that must be correctly and efficiently interlocked. Good hand-eye coordination is essential.

Computer versions of card games such as FreeCell and Solitaire require few skills and, like Tetris, people often play them out of boredom. Many corporate-cubicle drones play computer Solitaire. The fact that this card game holds more interest than many jobs should alarm anyone who owns or runs a business.

Puzzle games distract and lightly amuse, but rarely does anyone miss work or school because they just could not resist the urge to play Solitaire, Tetris, or Text Twist. However, I had a client—a college professor—who was so addicted to Solitaire that he removed the game from his computer and stored the disk in a safety deposit box!

Addiction risk for puzzle games: 2

Physical Simulations

As the latest arrivals to the video game universe, physical games are helping to remedy the physical inactivity that most often accompanies video game use. In Dance Dance Revolution (DDR), a player has to move his or her feet to a specific pattern while stepping in time to the beat of a song. Players work up a sweat, improve their rhythm, and learn dance skills at the same time. Similarly, Guitar Hero involves playing notes on a guitar to match up with the song being played. This game teaches hand-eye coordination and actually instructs users in musical theory. In fact, one of my students took lessons from a human instructor after playing the game. Finally, physical video simulations are available for a variety of sports, such as snowboarding, baseball, and bowling. One company has come out with a vest that allows players to feel the actual physical blows they may suffer in a game.

This category of games certainly can be addictive, but play time is significantly curtailed by the limitations imposed by physical exertion. I strongly recommend that homes with any video game system be outfitted with at least one physical game.

Addiction risk for physical simulations: 2

Old School Games

Older console games for systems such as Nintendo 64, PlayStation 1, and Sega's Dreamcast are just plain fun. They often involve cartoonlike characters in mazes, races, and battles. Families and friends can play together, creating an opportunity for social interaction. Other than fantasy role-playing games like Legend of Zelda and first-person shooter games like GoldenEye 007, offerings from these systems generally carry low potential for addiction. I highly recommend any of these slightly older video game systems.

As an aside, it may seem odd that the author of a book about video game addiction is recommending video games. I believe, however, that we need to learn to have a healthy relationship with video games, not remove them from our lives completely. The most overprotective of parents cannot shield their children from video games in a world where the games are everywhere.

Addiction risk for old school games: 3

Educational Games

Powerful educational games have proliferated recently. Teachers use interactive educational games with increasing frequency. Rather than lecture to students about life in the Third World, teachers may use Ayiti: The Cost of Life, which allows young people to take responsibility for a family of five in Haiti, with the goal of raising family income and living standards.[3] What a powerful way to learn about the world and what we can do to change it! Government and social studies teachers make use of a game platform called TheorySpark, which allows students to run election campaigns in different political systems. Such games provide an intense, hands-on learning experience.

Additionally, several of the games that were addictive for me (for example, Gettysburg!, Rome: Total War, and Age of Empires) offer very accurate historical representations and give players an in-depth education on historical periods. One teenage client reported that several such games he played had helped him significantly with history classes. Educational games have a mild risk for addiction, but this increases when the educational component is combined with other gaming elements (role play or real-time strategy, for instance, which will be discussed later in this chapter). Caution is advisable.

Addiction risk for educational games: 4

MY STORY: HOOKED ON HISTORY

The interactive, real-time, and global nature of online games hooked me powerfully in the late 1990s. Because I am a history nut, Sid Meier's Gettysburg! fired my imagination. Any game that Meier designs carries astronomical addictive potential for me. When I played the game, I was right there commanding my regiments when General Heth's division was making its way back to Gettysburg. General Buford and I, we stopped those rebels cold! The Confederates got close to McPherson's farm, but the grapeshot from our artillery taught them respect.

My fantasy of being a battlefield commander was once again fulfilled. I mastered the game engine and quickly could command an entire brigade to wheel left, right, and even to "refuse the flank," as Colonel Chamberlain had done on Little Round Top. I joined a clan that met online every night at eight o'clock and challenged other clans to bloody Civil War combat. We all played until at least one in the morning, but often some of us battled until it was time to go to work the next day. With people from all over the world playing, there was always fresh cannon fodder for my clan's insatiable urge to return to the battlefields of the 1860s. I was captivated by the historical realism of Gettysburg!, as well as the online camaraderie with my clan.

Manage and Control Games (God Games)

In this type of game, players control multiple aspects of the physical world. In The Sims, a life simulation module, players control the housing, finances, food intake, and relationship decisions of the characters in the game. In RollerCoaster Tycoon, a player makes decisions to construct, maintain, and grow an amusement park. In Black & White, players take on the role of a god and act to influence the lives of a group of islanders.

These games usually have no win-or-lose scenario, and the user does not directly control the characters. Players delight in controlling growth, development, and evolution, and any fan of a God Game enjoys the opportunity to exert complete dominance over the people and places in the game. These games do sometimes produce addicts, several of whom I have seen professionally.

Addiction risk for manage and control games: 5

Shoot 'Em Up and Adventure Games

With the games in this section, the chances of addiction increase dramatically. Players of these games experience an ever-deepening sense of connectedness to the characters they control. Higher levels of realism equal heightened sensory stimulation. The unceasing potential for new missions and adventures ensures that players do not quickly tire of these games.

First-Person Shooter (FPS) Games

FPS games rate as public enemy number one for many parents because of the incredible levels of violence that accompany them. This category includes many M-rated (mature-rated) games.

In an FPS, a player's view is much the same as in real life: players must constantly move their field of vision to see what is happening in their three-dimensional cyber world. FPS games require a high level of concentration as well as quick reflexes. Virtual death may be waiting around the next corner. Players make their way through mazes, cities, or battlefields to search out and destroy their enemies.

Counter-Strike is one of the more popular FPS games. Participants usually play online, with a small number of teammates on each side—terrorists versus antiterrorists. They fight house-to-house and street-to-street. In addition, many fans of Counter-Strike, Halo, and Call of Duty (which all have FPS modes of game play) form clans and meet online for team battles. Halo acquired such a dedicated following that throngs of devotees waited in line all night to purchase the first copies of Halo 3 upon its release in 2007. First-person shooters carry enormous risk for addiction, especially after a gamer joins a clan.

Addiction risk for first-person shooter games: 7

Real-Time Strategy (RTS) Games

RTS games involve building a civilization and amassing technology to advance to higher levels of development. At the same time, players must prepare an army for war against neighboring factions. Unlike in FPS games, RTS players control an entire battlefield as well as make overall strategic decisions. Success at these games requires skill at multitasking. A player manages an economy, controls armies, and in some cases, keeps the peasants happy or faces revolt.

The RTS genre of games grew out of turn-based strategy games like Sid Meier's Civilization, which are much less intense. Examples of RTS games include Age of Empires, Empire Earth, and Command & Conquer. They can be played alone, but several online multiplayer engines facilitate group gaming with players from all over the world. RTS games carry enormous risk of addiction and are often "gateway games," those games that rapidly increase the pace toward addiction. Players who derive satisfaction from the online multiplayer feature of these games often crave greater interaction and connection with other players than RTS games can supply.

Online RTS games pit small numbers of players against each other, and interaction between team members while playing is fairly limited. RTS games whet players' appetites for greater complexity of online interaction.

Addiction risk for real-time strategy games: 7

Adventure and Role-Playing Games (RPGs)

This category also contains many gateway games because players of this genre seem to quite easily move to the more addictive MMORPGs (discussed later). Adventure and role-playing games draw discovery-oriented players and, as is obvious from their name, those motivated by role playing.

In RPGs, a player acts as a fantasy character and embarks on a quest that progresses through many trials and obstacles, usually toward a goal, which could be anything from saving the princess to finding the Holy Grail. In some games, there is no ultimate goal, no win-or-lose scenario, but rather simply an opportunity to exist as the character, occasionally happening upon discovery and adventure. A player's choices help shape the direction of the game, a fact which also appeals to control-oriented gamers. Examples include Legend of Zelda, Final Fantasy, and Warhammer. Potential for addiction is high.

Addiction risk for adventure and role-playing games: 8

The Narcotics of the Game World: MMORPGs

Are you bored with your life? Does the daily grind weigh heavily upon you? Well, Massively Multiplayer Online Role-Playing Games (MMORPGs) may be able to help.

These wildly popular recent additions to the video game universe are played by tens of millions of people across the world. Each player controls an avatar, or fantasy character. Players choose the race, class, and sometimes even the profession of the avatar. They interact with each other in persistent worlds that operate twenty-four hours a day. With many of these games, someone, somewhere, is playing every minute of every day.

Players join clans and guilds of like-minded avatars. They cooperate on quests and adventures, and even chat with each other through headsets. They often experience a bond with their fantasy friends that transcends any they have had before. They venture into dungeons together and support each other through repeated trials. Tests of martial, magical, and cooperative skills await them on a daily basis. Many players of MMORPGs think about the game constantly and cannot wait to return to the portal of their computer screen at the end of a work or school day. MMORPGs possess the power to shift perception. A strongly addicted player relates to this online world as *the* real world and his or her other life as simply a necessary evil. His or her time, money, and emotional resources get sucked in by the game. MMORPGs—of which there are now nearly two hundred in existence—carry the most destructive potential of any video game genre I have encountered.

Relationships, career, and family could all very well suffer. If you or a loved one play an MMORPG, please exercise extreme caution. Confronting an MMORPG addict often requires professional intervention.

RuneScape

RuneScape counts over ten million active users, primarily because 90 percent of RuneScape players use the free version of the game. In a month's time, over ten million different users log on and play the game.[4] RuneScape takes place in a fantasy realm called Gielinor, which is subdivided into distinct kingdoms and territories. Players can customize their avatars. They collect resources, purchase upgrades, engage in combat, and are motivated by increasing the level and experience of their avatar.

RuneScape worries me not because of its own addictive potential, but rather because I have witnessed players of this MMORPG go on to other, more powerful game engines. RuneScape generally appeals to younger players, primarily between the ages of nine and fifteen. If you discover that your loved one plays this game, it might be time to have a serious talk so as to head off future addiction.

Addiction risk for RuneScape: 7

World of Warcraft (WoW)

World of Warcraft counts more than nine million users internationally. Gamers pay $13 to $15 each month, and the first month comes free. The constantly running game engine owes much of its success to its unceasing opportunities for discovery, exploration, and conquest. WoW appeals to a diverse array of gaming motivations and draws players away from many other game types. The game appeals to role players, adventurers, and fantasy-oriented individuals. It also offers players a vast online social network, making those who lack friends easy prey to the game's addictive influence.

WoW aficionados almost always join guilds. Guild members goad each other into showing up online because success in many quests and dungeons requires a large number of cooperating players. If a guild member does not log on at the appointed time, he or she is letting down the team. This social pressure serves to suck players into ever-increasing expenditures of time. Many WoW fans feel a familial allegiance to members of their team, a feature that plays an integral part in WoW's ability to take over players' lives.

Patience is one trait all WoW players share. The people who succeed in WoW are those who spend the most time playing it. It's that simple. The person who controls a powerful avatar with incredible armor and an awesome two-handed axe has acquired those attributes over hundreds or sometimes thousands of hours of play.

In the initial levels of the game, rewards, items, and upgrades come quickly. However, as players "level up" and move to higher quests and dungeons, rewards begin to require massive amounts of game time to obtain. A game designer who wishes to maximize addictive potential should follow this facet of WoW's design. The game's addictive progression mirrors, in many ways, the patterns of addiction found with drug abuse. As an example, a childhood friend of mine has struggled with crack cocaine. He once told me, "The first time I did crack, it was like an awesome hurricane was happening all over my body. It never felt that good again, but the memory of the experience kept me using crack because I thought I would someday get back to the incredible high that I had my first time." WoW users experience euphoria and deep satisfaction when they complete a quest or acquire some new attribute. Positive feedback from other players and memory of the euphoria drive them to keep at the game so they can keep advancing and keep experiencing those "wonderful feelings."

WoW accounts for roughly one in three people I see professionally. The most difficult task I have is convincing a WoW addict that he or she has a problem. These individuals must often hit absolute bottom—realizing they have completely lost control over their lives—before they accept anything I say. WoW addicts talk about the game as if their activities within the game were real. They often completely lose touch with reality.

To make matters worse, several of my clients have admitted to me that they use marijuana and megadoses of caffeine to enhance their ability to lose themselves in the game. "With weed," one college-aged client confessed, "I completely and thoroughly merge with the game." As he described it, time spent on the game comes close to being an out-of-body experience.

I have seen this disturbing marriage of drugs and video games with another MMORPG called EverQuest. Many players jokingly refer to the game as EverCrack. It shares many similarities to WoW, but EverQuest has been decreasing in popularity, largely due to WoW's mass appeal.

Addiction risk for World of Warcraft: 10

Relationships and the World of Warcraft

Many video gamers develop what they consider deep friendships within their online clans, teams, and guilds. One young woman, Lisa, a World of Warcraft addict, came to see me after an online romance turned ugly. Her "Draenei" avatar fell in love with his "Night Elf." These two characters are from races within the game that players can choose from. They are similar to characters from the *Lord of the Rings* trilogy. Lisa had chatted online for months with the man and, as she put it, "We were perfect for each other." They decided to take a trip together to Las Vegas. Twenty-one-year-old Lisa was certain that the twenty-eight-year-old unemployed factory worker who lived in his mother's basement would soon be her husband.

She learned quickly that the outgoing and compassionate "Night Elf" was only a persona, the opposite of this man's true nature. "He couldn't even look me in the eye," Lisa told me, still in disbelief. "I can't believe I was so stupid." Games—and online social networking—can absorb some players to such an extent that they lose the ability to differentiate between real relationships and those based in fantasy. Lisa confused successful online communication with the real thing. She stopped playing World of Warcraft only to become a MySpace maven, putting in four to five hours a night on updating and editing her page as well as adding to and keeping up with her network.

Video game designers have taken note of WoW's incredible success using avatars. The latest version of Call of Duty, a first-person shooter World War II combat game, allows players to customize an avatar and thereby amass experience points, gain new weapons, and advance through the ranks. This "avatarization" takes a game that already had a high risk for addiction and drastically increases it.

As the appeal of all video games continues its meteoric rise, video game addiction will become much more commonplace. Likewise, as the popularity of social networking sites and real-time online chatting continue to grow exponentially, Internet-based addictive behavior will increase dramatically.

Blurring the Lines

In this book, video gaming and Internet-based activities are viewed as two related, but distinct, phenomena. However, technological trends have blurred these lines. People who are drawn to one type of cyber technology are likely to be drawn to others.

This makes cyber-based addictions particularly pernicious because when one type of addictive activity is brought under control, there are others that quickly pop up.

Social networking sites offer numerous applications, many of which look very much like video games. For example, applications such as FarmVille and Mafia Wars are occasional amusements for most who play them, but for some, they become downright obsessions. Mafia Wars, which can be played on MySpace, Facebook, or Friendster, is set in the Little Italy neighborhood of New York City. The game focuses on mastering "jobs" to amass money and experience in order to establish and move forward a player's criminal empire. Players also expand their own crime "families" by recruiting other players. As with online multiplayer games such as World of Warcraft, some Mafia Wars aficionados form clans—crime organizations with hundreds, perhaps even thousands, that war against other clans. Much like real mafia families, clans in the game put out hits on each others' members. This gives the game a decidedly social quality which in turn exacerbates the tendency for participants to excessively game.

With images and jargon that most people know from iconic mob movies such as *The Godfather, Casino,* and *GoodFellas,* Mafia Wars shows how the lines between movies, pop culture, video games, and social networking have become blurred. The worlds of media, entertainment, and electronic recreation seem to be on a collision course with ever-increasing speed.

Given that these applications can be accessed through a smartphone and played all day at home, work, and school, the cyber addict has little trouble accessing his or her favorite compulsions. It used to be that indulging addictive urges often required a certain degree of effort. It takes a good deal of energy, planning, and money, for example, to buy illicit drugs or go to the store to purchase alcohol. For the cyber addict, the addictive behavior is accessed effortlessly with the click of a button, making this problem even more insidious.

Smartphones are particularly troublesome because they represent, for the addictively prone person, a densely packed and totally mobile platform of addictive temptations. If a person has an addictive relationship with Facebook that is successfully dealt with and stopped, there are dozens of other applications on the phone with the potential to tantalize and take the person down another addictive path. I have urged most of my clients to get rid of smartphones for these reasons.

The Next Step

The lines between video gaming and Internet-based addictions have been obscured, revealing the reality that people prone to cyber addiction are being bombarded by an increasing array of temptations. I believe that the propensity to become addicted resides in the hardwiring of our brains and in our early familial experiences. Thus, those who seek to recover from addiction of any sort most likely have a good deal of personal growth work to do to understand what it is about them that makes them at risk for addiction. They also need to develop an enduring program of recovery to head off becoming entrapped in another addiction once the primary addictive behavior is stopped.

We turn now in the next chapter to tackle the first part of this assertion by showing how addiction and the functioning of the brain are intimately related.

CHAPTER 3

your brain in cyberland

"Science progresses best when observations
force us to alter our preconceptions."
Vera Rubin, astronomer

I lost a job because I consistently showed up late. Gaming into
the wee hours cut into my sleep, so I never could get up on time.
When I first stopped gaming, I continued short-changing my
sleep by marathon online chatting sessions with people all over
the world. I hated myself for this irresponsible behavior, but
nevertheless, I would go home from work and start playing my
game the minute I walked in the door, and later opening multiple
instant messenger systems. I wanted a different kind of life, but
not enough, apparently, to make me escape this destructive cycle.
I have since learned that the disconnect between what I wanted
and how I behaved may have stemmed from the fact that my
brain had gone haywire.

The role of the brain in addiction and compulsive behaviors is
complex. In this chapter, I outline the basics of what science has
learned about addiction, explaining the interplay between addictive behavior and the workings of the brain. As much as possible,
I have tried to translate current scientific theories and research
into layman's terms.

Brain Disorders

Alcoholism and drug addiction have long been considered pro-
gressive diseases—that is, they worsen with time. The same

can be said for gaming and Internet addictions. What begins as fairly benign activity will, for the addict, continue to progress into out-of-control behavior with severe consequences. The impulse to indulge in an addictive substance or behavior becomes overpowering, feeling less like a desire and more like an absolute need. Many people believe that addicts simply lack willpower. These folks see the addict as morally flawed, whereas professionals in the field of addiction view an addict as someone with a chronic brain disorder.[1]

CAN'T THEY JUST STOP?

"Why can't you *just stop*?" nonaddicts will often ask. When you ask us to stop gaming or to give up online social networking, you might as well ask that we stop living. The circuits of our brains have become intertwined in the characters and events of our magical reality. The games and our social networking profiles become veritable extensions of ourselves. We chase rewards in our games and amass friends in our online networks with the same intensity that people pursue food when they are hungry. The cyber world completely absorbs the motivational circuitry of our minds. When you attempt to help a cyber addict, you must realize that you are battling fundamental forces within his or her brain.

Science now tells us that both the makeup and the changes that occur in an addict's brain are at play with addiction. Indeed, over the last twenty years, scientists have discovered how changes in the brain lead to addiction. In the last few years, researchers have shown that compulsive Internet and video game use can induce the same changes in the brain as does alcohol or marijuana.[2] Although research specifically on gaming and Internet addiction is still limited, results from research on these cyber activities is starting to come in, and we can learn much from examining what science has already confirmed about other behavioral and substance addictions. Indeed, a vast body of scientific evidence shows that genes involved in addiction are not specific to alcoholism or drug dependence, but are involved in all behavioral addictions.[3]

Compulsive Internet use and video game play exhibit the same "signature" in the brain as other addictions.[4] As far as the brain is concerned, an addictive reward is a reward, whether it comes from a chemical (alcohol and other drugs) or an experience (gambling, the Internet, or video games, for instance).[5]

The brain of an addict has features that distinguish it from that of a nonaddict. These features can be observed from changes in brain activity.[6] Sophisticated scanning technology, such as positron emission tomography (PET) and magnetic resonance imaging (MRI), allows scientists to measure the activity of certain areas of the brain and determine how those areas carry out their required roles. Some scanning techniques measure brain waves, and others measure blood flow and metabolism in the brain. Under a scan, the brain of an addict looks distinctly different from that of a nonaddict.[7]

ADDICTION CHANGES THE BRAIN

Repeated exposure to a drug or behavior permanently changes the brains of addicts. In technical terms, specific brain neurons (nerve cells) change as a result of such exposure.[8] The brain simply adapts to the new chemical environment caused by the addictive substance or behavior.[9] Some areas of the brain become more active, while other areas stagnate. Since the brain controls the way we behave, the addicted person starts acting differently. The brain is a vastly intricate highway of neural roads and networks. Addiction floods some roads with increased traffic, while allowing other roads to fall into disuse and disrepair.

Scientists studying addiction using rats in a laboratory report the characteristic addiction-related alterations in the rats' brains.[10] Willpower and morality play no role in the rats becoming full-fledged addicts. Addiction brings out these changes in the brain.

All addictive behaviors and substances affect two pathways deep in the brain.[11] These are called the mesolimbic and mesocortical pathways. Think of these technical terms as different roads that lead to Las Vegas, one of the world's great pleasure capitals (and a mecca for many addicts!).

To arrive at pleasure, you pretty much have to take one of these two roads. There is a special vehicle that gets you there. The vehicle is called dopamine, a chemical that rides these roads to activate the pleasure centers, which are areas in the brain that control our feelings of pleasure.[12] Scientists refer to these pathways as the brain's reward system.[13] If you go to Las Vegas and you have a good time, that's rewarding. As a result, you'll probably want to go back. When something is pleasurable, you want it to happen again. When the rewarding behavior happens again and you get pleasure again, the behavior becomes reinforced. After that, you'll probably tell all your friends and try to get them to join you in Vegas!

When rewarding behaviors are reinforced again and again, the brain develops powerful motivation to repeat them. In an addict, this desire stays strong even when the behavior produces negative consequences.[14] Urge overpowers reason.

MY BRAIN WON'T LET ME STOP

Even when addicts manage to stop one addictive behavior or substance, they often switch to another. Once a person crosses into addiction, it becomes extraordinarily difficult for him or her to turn back because of the changes that have taken place in the brain.

Repeated use seems to create a switch in the brain.[15] Initially, compulsions such as drug use, excessive Internet use, and video game play are voluntary behaviors, but when that switch is thrown, the user or player moves into the state of addiction, characterized by fix-seeking behavior.[16] In other words, behaviors that end up becoming addictive do not start that way. At some point, a threshold is reached, and the brain converts voluntary behavior to something totally involuntary—the brain itself becomes addicted. It remembers those feelings of pleasure and demands that they be repeated.

Once the switch to addiction is thrown, self-discipline exerts little influence.[17] When researchers stimulate the memory area in the brain of a rat that previously kicked the cocaine habit, the rat will desperately begin to look for a fix.[18] Stimulating the area of the brain that produces the high itself—the pleasure center—has little effect in reigniting addictive behavior.[19] It becomes important, therefore, for the addict not only to avoid the addictive behavior itself, but also situations that cause him or her to recall the "good feelings" the addictive behavior produced.

Memories of pleasure activate a desire to attain it. Potentially, anything that triggers memory can take the recovering addict into relapse. Obviously, if you are a recovering alcoholic, you probably want to stay out of bars. Even so, you still find yourself bombarded with images on television and in magazines of smiling people consuming alcohol. Recovering cyber addicts will find computers and game consoles all around them—constant reminders of pleasure that make recovery increasingly difficult.

THE CIRCUITS OF ADDICTION

The pathways of addiction lie deep within the brain. Going back to our Las Vegas analogy on the road to pleasure, we can compare neurons to small towns along the way. Travel along the road is basically stopping at one small town after another until you hit Vegas. To get between these neurons—our small towns—you need a neurotransmitter, which is any chemical that transmits messages (electrical impulses) from one neuron to another. Sending messages also involves receptors, which receive the messages, and transporters, which are part of the nerve cells that send the message.

The various kinds of neurotransmitters work in different ways. In the real world, if you have to send a package that absolutely must be there overnight, you'd use a reliable shipping service. If you need to send money to your son who lost his wallet on a trip in Argentina, you'd use a reliable wire transfer service. If you need an inexpensive method to send wedding invitations, you'd use postal mail. In this same way, different neurotransmitters are linked with specific parts of the brain and have different, specific functions. For our purposes, we are going to focus on dopamine. In addition to its many other functions, dopamine will expedite you directly to the pleasure centers of Las Vegas.

DOPAMINE DELIVERS

Although many aspects of brain chemistry are involved in addiction, the neurotransmitter dopamine plays a key role. Dopamine is a natural chemical in our bodies, a messenger that lets us know we find a certain activity pleasurable. Dopamine also plays a central role in emotional stability and mood regulation.[20] Our brains experience an increase in dopamine levels whenever we do something that makes us feel good and even when we begin a process that will lead to a pleasurable goal or experience. Indeed, the anticipatory phase of a goal triggers dopamine levels to rise.[21] It is this natural process of dopamine delivery that gets messed up through addictions. We've known for a while that increased levels of dopamine are linked with cocaine, amphetamine, and marijuana use, as well as with alcohol and nicotine addiction.[22] Now scientists are observing these same increased dopamine levels with behavioral addictions such as gambling, Internet use, and video gaming. And it is not just the actual behavior or substance that leads to changes; simply thinking about the behavior causes dopamine levels to increase.[23] This finding certainly rings true with my personal experience—my mood changed whenever I anticipated going home to play my game.

Again, the natural role of dopamine in our brains is to reinforce positive experiences, making us want to repeat them. When an addictive substance or behavior is involved, however, this motivation goes into overdrive. According to Jaak Panksepp, a neuroscientist at the Falk Center for Molecular Therapeutics at Northwestern University, the dopamine system is the brain's seeking circuitry, which impels us to explore new possibilities for reward.[24] He writes, "The game world is teeming with objects that deliver clearly articulated rewards: more life, access to new levels, new equipment, new spells. Most of the crucial work in game interface design revolves around keeping players notified of potential rewards available to them and how much those rewards are needed."[25] In this way, video games activate our brain's reward system.

The possibility for increasingly satisfying rewards and exploration directly affects dopamine levels. As the behavior gets reinforced with a surge of dopamine, some players begin to relate to the game in an increasingly compulsive manner. Successful video game designers certainly exploit this dopamine-mediated reality. Whether this is their intention or not, it is the result.

Although most of the research on the role of the brain in addiction has focused on substance abuse, gambling, or overeating, recent scientific studies point to drastic increases in dopamine levels from cyber addictions as well.[26] In one study, the human brain was shown to release dopamine while participants were playing video games that involved shooting enemy tanks.[27] The tank-killing success of the player was proportional to the amount of dopamine released. A greater number of "kills," going to the next level, or gaining more experience points all add up to more dopamine. Another study showed great success in treating cyber-based addiction with a medication called naltrexone that acts on the brain's reward system and has been used in treating alcoholism.[28] When this drug was combined with a serotonin reuptake inhibitor (antidepressant), addictive cyber-urges and behavior declined significantly.

The dopamine connection with compulsive video game play was also examined in a June 2007 study. Scientists who used an encephalograph (another machine used to measure brain activity) on study participants found increased activity in the pleasure centers of those who played video games to excess.[29] These individuals also were found to have significantly heightened emotional reactions to their game play compared to noncompulsive gamers.[30] For this group of people, gaming is a much more intense and involved activity than it is for the general population.

These findings further demonstrate that video gaming is a bona fide addiction, which can be placed under the umbrella of a cyber-based behavioral addiction.

Our Genes Do Play a Role

But, you may say, not everyone who plays video games, sends texts, or surfs the Internet becomes addicted. That's most certainly true, and again our brains as well as genetics seem to explain why. Some people are simply at higher risk of developing an addiction. Looking at my family tree, I have no doubt that I was born with an elevated risk for addiction. Alcohol, marijuana, crack, gambling, and food addiction are some of the known substances and compulsive behaviors that have been problematic or addictive for my family members.

While anyone who derives great pleasure from cyber-based behaviors is experiencing an increase of dopamine, compulsive players have brains that make them more vulnerable to craving the dopamine-induced high. These folks are very susceptible to addiction, then, because their dopamine receptors do not work properly, and some individuals simply have fewer dopamine receptors.[31] Although scientists do not fully understand the mechanism involved, low levels of dopamine receptors increase a person's likelihood of becoming addicted, whether to a behavior or a substance. People with normal levels of these receptors do not get the intense feelings of pleasure that an individual with low levels does.

Variation in certain structures in the brain is much more well-documented with ADHD. Recent studies also suggest that people with ADHD are not only at significantly increased risk for substance abuse,[32] but also for cyber addictions.[33] Individuals with ADHD have DNA differences that make them much more susceptible to the addictive allure of cyberland.

Some strains of rats, for example, seem more inclined to become addicts than others. Not all rats can be induced to develop a drug addiction, even with repeated exposure. But in some rats, the path to addiction is quick and easy. In the case of addiction, what's true for rats is also true for humans. The varying degrees of vulnerability are believed to result from genetic factors, meaning that some of us are just more susceptible.

Current research studies claim to correlate 50 to 60 percent of addiction to genetics.[34] Many studies demonstrate that if one of your parents is an alcoholic, your chances of becoming an alcoholic increase by one third; if both parents are alcoholic, your chances quadruple.[35] The studies that examine genetic predisposition to addiction have centered primarily on alcoholism, but given the similarities among all addictions, it is not a stretch to propose that one's genes may also heavily influence whether an individual becomes a cyber addict.

One study showed a particular serotonin transporter gene variant that is prevalent among cyber addicts. The gene, called 5HTTLPR, appears much more frequently in people who meet the criteria for excessive Internet use.[36] Serotonin is a neurotransmitter involved in depression, and the study also suggested that cyber junkies often struggle with this menacing condition alongside their addiction.[37] Scientific study is ongoing, as researchers try to pinpoint more specific differences in the brains of cyber addicts.

DNA, however, is not destiny.[38] Even people whose brains and genetic makeup put them at high risk for developing an addiction may not ever do so. Studies of identical twins support this idea: despite matching DNA, their heights, need for glasses, disease susceptibilities, or personalities may differ.[39] How genes reveal themselves varies with different environments, and even within the same environment. The interaction between genes and the environment will certainly receive greater attention in the future.

MY STORY: A FAMILY OF ADDICTS AND ENABLERS

For clarification, an addict is someone who is psychologically and/or physiologically dependent on a substance or behavior. Someone who is an enabler or codependent, on the other hand, gives material aid and provides excuses that permit addicted individuals to avoid the consequences of their self-destructive behaviors. My family is full of both types of individuals.

My sister performed an exhaustive genealogical study of our family, which took her several years to complete. Anecdotes of addiction abounded—a recurring pattern that lay behind many of our family's tragedies. My sister's research showed me that my genes and family history predisposed me to addiction. Owing to a streak of good fortune and powerful mentors, I never became a substance addict. I credit this with the constant reminders from my mother, the powerful support from my sisters, and extraordinary mentoring. However, as I relay my story throughout the pages of this book, you can see that these protective factors were not able to keep me from developing a cyber addiction.

"I'VE GOT TO LOG ON NOW!"

As a video game user progresses from casual to compulsive use, the communication system in his or her brain's reward system goes haywire. Feel-good dopamine levels are elevated much of the time, and yet cravings intensify. As the individual becomes addicted, the drive to repeat the cyber or gaming experience becomes entangled in the same brain circuits as those for eating, sex, and survival. Our brains are hardwired to pursue certain rewards because of their survival value.[40]

This neurochemical reality can be found in nature. Dopamine levels "are at their highest when an animal is actively seeking food, a safe place, or a mate."[41] When we learn that a blizzard is on its way, we stock up on supplies and necessities.[42] As animals perceive the onset of cooler weather, they busy themselves—under the influence of elevated dopamine levels—in collecting food or preparing their winter dens.

This same sense of urgency becomes linked in an addict's mind to the acquisition of a drug or the acting out of a behavior such as playing video games. To the addict, it feels as though the addictive behavior is necessary for survival.

When addictive impulses become entwined in that survival circuitry, the addicted individual experiences strong cravings, just like any animal does for food or sex. Ronald Ruden, author of *The Craving Brain*, captures the biological reality of this situation:

> Craving is an extreme biological response. Desire, want, and need are normal biological responses without the obsessional features that define craving. Originally, craving was a response that only occurred when survival was at stake . . . The pain produced by this system was intense, allowing only those thoughts that would remove the pain.[43]

When an addict fails to find a fix, he or she often experiences agony. Some experts on addiction say that addictive substances and behaviors hijack the brain and its survival circuitry.

We all crave food when we are very hungry; without nourishment we would die. This is one of nature's ways of ensuring our survival. Addiction incorrectly links the addictive behavior with our drive to survive. Such linkage explains why the behavior of addicts seems inexplicable and irrational to nonaddicts. In addiction, the need to satisfy the craving rises to the intensity of our need to survive. That is one of the main reasons that addiction is incredibly difficult to reverse.

An addict's brain often shows reduced activity in the prefrontal region, a part of the brain in which rational thought can override impulsive behavior.[44] This area of the brain, characteristically underactive in individuals with ADHD, is also one of the last to develop, a fact which helps explain the prevalence of cyber addiction among those with ADHD and adolescents. Thus, an addict may also lack the ability to override his or her behavior with rational thought. The addict's brain is telling him or her that in order to survive, he or she must indulge in the addiction. The behavior is irrational to everyone but the addict, for whom the behavior is simply a matter of survival.

AN HOUR A DAY OF CYBER ACTIVITY TURNS INTO TEN

Along with intense cravings, addictions are also characterized by what experts call tolerance. Tolerance means that over time, an addict requires more of the substance or behavior to get the same high. Although each addictive drug or behavior has its own particular effects, all bombard the brain's dopamine reward circuits.[45] Long-term use reduces the number of receptors that are activated by dopamine as well as the natural production of this important neurotransmitter, thus creating a need for in-creasing levels of the addictive behavior to satisfy the craving.[46] This reality means that addicts must engage in ever-increasing amounts of the behavior to achieve the same feeling or reward. (See chapter 4 for more information on tolerance.)

The Next Step

It's not critical that you remember the details of the brain chemistry discussed in this chapter. Rather, the most important information to take away is that addiction is a brain disorder. If you see a family member sitting at the computer or at a game console for hours on end, know that the behavior you used to call simply excessive may be an addiction. You must recognize that you are dealing with a condition of the brain, one that needs intervention and treatment.

It is important to understand, as well, that addiction to one substance or behavior increases the likelihood that the individual will succumb to other addictive compulsions. As a society, we watch our loved ones for the warning signs of substance abuse. It is time that we paid equal attention to the behavioral patterns associated with the cyber world.

The developments in the science of brain addiction help us understand how gaming and other cyber activities can progress into out-of-control addictions. We also know that there is more to the story of how addiction develops, including our genetic makeup, our environment, and our individual behavior. This combination of factors influences how vulnerable we are to cyber addiction. In the next chapter, we'll look at what happens when a cyber compulsion takes hold.

CHAPTER 4

into the black hole

"An addict can be an Olympic gold medalist, an army general,
or a multimillion-dollar professional baseball player."
Ronald Ruden, author of *The Craving Brain*

Problematic cyber use cuts across all socioeconomic, ethnic, religious, and age groups. My clients who face these issues have ranged from corporate executives to factory workers, college students, middle school students, and even a Catholic priest. All these folks exhibit what has been called a "persistent, compulsive dependence"[1] on their particular cyber behavior.

The concept of dependence captures the reality that an addict thinks that he or she requires the game or other cyber activity to survive. As we discussed in chapter 3, the addiction has become wired into the addict's brain. Researchers speak of two main types of addiction: substance addiction (alcohol, street drugs, nicotine) and process addiction (excessive amounts of gambling, sex, shopping, eating, Internet use).[2] As with food, gambling, sex, and shopping, most of us can hang out in cyberland without a problem. For others, cyber compulsions morph into an impulse control disorder or an addiction.[3]

This chapter will describe patterns of cyber activity that may indicate the user is spiraling into the black hole of addiction. It recounts my personal journey from normal play into out-of-control use. It also provides a checklist to help you determine if it's time to seek professional help for your cyber use or that of your loved one.

Headed for Trouble

As video games crept into my life in middle school, we were still playing Atari, ColecoVision, and Intellivision.

When I was around eleven or twelve years old, my friend Tim had the new Atari. The neighborhood kids congregated at his house starting with the first day of summer. We were excited and felt privileged to be allowed there and to experience the cutting-edge video game technology.

For almost a week, four or five of us passed whole days at Tim's house. We took turns supplying the snack food, and we all chipped in for pizza. Tim's mother quickly became alarmed at our sedentary ways and at first pleasantly suggested that we might have more fun if we played some baseball outside. Eventually, when we refused her gentle suggestions, she banned all kids from the house except for one hour a day and severely limited Tim's game time.

Although some parents were leery of the new electronic forms of recreation and restricted our use of them, the games back then actually quickly became tiresome and were self-limiting. It was the early to mid-1980s, and the game systems and technology of this era were fairly primitive. It didn't take a great deal of video game acumen to beat the game, and advancement through the different levels went by with predictable ease. The games lacked the interactive quality of today's games, and playing a two-player game with a group of friends meant you had to take turns and spend a lot of time waiting. There was no chance that I would get my own game system, as my mother—like many parents—was suspicious of the new form of recreation and refused to buy one. She correctly surmised that such a purchase promised to lead me into an inactive lifestyle. Thus, I was relegated to friends' houses to indulge. My mother's wisdom prevented me from getting the gaming bug for many years.

THE HOOK: MY LOVE OF HISTORY—FRIEND AND FOE

My love of history proved to be my Achilles' heel. Some younger neighbor kids had a Sega Genesis system with graphics that were greatly enhanced over the likes of Atari. I was home from college for the summer, and these kids' mother needed someone to stay with them during the day, so I agreed.

I became somewhat of a surrogate big brother and thrilled them with my mastery of one glorious game, Centurion: Defender of Rome. This multidimensional game allowed players to become a Roman official, work their way up the ranks, and, if successful, end up as commander of many Roman legions. I battled the Gauls, the Carthaginians, and the Parthian invaders. I became a master charioteer and bribed Roman officials, ultimately being crowned the caesar of the empire!

I was so taken with the game that I would play for seven or eight hours straight. I would watch those kids whenever I was asked, as long as I could have at that game. I thought all day long about playing it and hungered to be caesar. I was no longer imagining military conquest—I was in the center of it! The game was magical, fulfilling my history-based fantasies in ways I had not dreamed possible.

HAIL CAESAR!

The more I played, the more my desire to keep playing deepened. The neighbor family was about to leave on a two-week trip up north. "Oh my God," I panicked. "How am I going to deal with two weeks of no game?" I had to have that game. The thought of not having it filled me with dread. I needed it, or at least I was convinced that I did.

Faced with such a long absence from my precious game, I willingly, if not desperately, offered to take care of the family's cat. Although they had planned on putting him in a kennel, they loved the idea that they could save money and be assured that the cat would receive some attention while they were gone. The cat would have gotten attention only if they had taken the Sega Genesis with them. When I was in the house, the cat was merely an afterthought. I filled two or three bowls with Friskies, filled a large water bowl, and let the cat fend for himself.

I slept at the neighbors' house on the floor in front of the television. I stayed up until four or five in the morning playing the game, went to sleep for a few hours, and then got up only to play until I could no longer keep my eyes open. I could have taken the game system to my house, but that would have meant dealing with my mother, who would never have put up with the incessant gaming.

Playing the game at the neighbors' house gave me a secret lair of video game serenity, the perfect flop house with creature comforts about which all addicts dream. I would be uninterrupted and left to pursue video game bliss. I remember waking up one morning and thinking of the Roman masses cheering, "Hail caesar!" I thought that I would have made a great Roman emperor, and the game gave me a chance to test my skills.

WHAT HAPPENS IF YOU BEAT THE GAME?

The great thing about Centurion: Defender of Rome was that it had multiple levels of difficulty. After I became caesar on one level, I would simply up the ante and play the next highest level. It took me the whole two weeks that my neighbors were on vacation to defeat all the levels.

Eventually I mastered the highest level, emperor. After my accomplishment, I was elated and deeply satisfied for about a day. These pleasant feelings gave way to depression because my fix was gone, but I still craved it. I later learned that it was the leveling up that held the thrill with this type of game. I had won every chariot race, subdued every province, and defeated the strongest of the barbarian hordes. No challenges were left. My daily thrill-of-victory fix was thus eliminated.

I tried playing the game again, handicapping myself in various ways to make it more challenging, but it wasn't the same. The allure was gone. The reward had been in being able to go to the next level, and there were no new levels left to conquer.

Now my motivation in general lagged, and instead of doing the errands and preparation I needed to get ready to go back to school, I moped around the house and watched television in a sort of stupor. The kids I had babysat kept calling, wondering why I hadn't been coming over. I didn't know what to tell them, so I just said I wasn't feeling well.

A few weeks later I returned to college, and the busyness of the semester brought me out of my post–video game doldrums. I had the good sense that year to avoid games, and as a result I performed well in school. I was not bitten again by the video game bug for quite a while. But technology continued to advance and these new tantalizing possibilities would one day drag me deeper into addiction than I could have ever imagined.

The Hallmarks of Addiction

A cyber addict loses the ability to choose. He or she continues cyber behaviors in spite of negative consequences and a strong desire to stop. Trouble soon manifests itself as the cyber world consumes the player's life. And because cyber junkies, like most addicts, usually hide their addictive behavior, detecting the problem in its early stages can be very difficult.

In my seminars, I distribute a list of warning signs for cyber addictions to help loved ones and possible addicts recognize troubling behaviors. I developed this list from my professional experience and current addiction literature, as well as from conversations with colleagues all over the country. If you or a loved one has exhibited four or more of the following behaviors for more than three months, it is time to seek professional help.

Warning Signs of Cyber Addiction[4]

1. Time warp—inability to determine time spent on gaming/cyber activities
2. Lying about gaming/cyber activities
3. Changes or disruptions in sleep patterns
4. Craving games/cyber activities

5. Withdrawing from family and friends

6. Losing interest in other hobbies and recreational activities

7. Gaming/Internet use for more than two hours a day, more than four days a week

8. Poor performance in school or at work

9. Physical ailments: backache, carpal tunnel syndrome, stiff neck, nerve pain, eyestrain

10. Inability to see the negative consequences of gaming/cyber activity

11. Buying game items or skills with real money

12. Eating meals at the computer

13. Glorifying gaming/cyber activity

14. Emotional disturbance when games/electronic devices are taken away

15. Mood swings

16. Withdrawal symptoms after playing games/cyber activity: headache, malaise, light-headedness

17. Continued gaming/cyber activity despite serious adverse consequences

18. Persistent inability to cut down on gaming/cyber activity

19. Ever-increasing amounts of time spent gaming/engaging in cyber activity

20. Obsessing about gaming/cyber activity even when not playing/online

---

Again, four or more of these characteristics exhibited persistently for more than three months should trigger an alarm. Discovering the problem early makes a great difference in the success of treatment. Like other addictions, if cyber addiction is left to fester, it can destroy the player's life.

Video game and other cyber addictions progress in a pattern similar to other, more widely studied addictions. The person feels a high from playing or using and, with time, the hours required to attain that high increase. The budding addict tries to cut down, but cannot. Soon the normal aspects of his or her life begin to suffer. Performance at work or school suffers. Relationships deteriorate because of the addict's increasing focus on the game or cyber activity. In spite of the negative consequences, the addict continues to play or engage in cyber activity.

Researchers who study Internet-based addictions often divide them into two categories: generalized and specific.[5] *Generalized Internet addiction* refers to someone who has an excessive/compulsive relationship with many aspects of the Internet, perhaps social networking sites, email, online chatting, or online forums. *Specific Internet addiction* refers to compulsive behavior with one particular aspect or application, such as Facebook. *Cyber-relational addiction* applies to people who turn away from family and friends in favor of cyber-relationships, while *cybersexual addiction* refers to compulsive downloading, watching, or trading online pornographic content.[6] One thing that all cyber addictions—and all addictions in general—share is that the time spent on the activity tends to increase over time.

AN HOUR A DAY USED TO BE ENOUGH: TOLERANCE

"Once I get on, I just can't get off the game, even though I really want to," Darryl confessed to me. Darryl, a good friend, has struggled with EverQuest, one of those highly addictive MMORPGs. He, like many players, calls it EverCrack.

The game has a seventy-five-level hierarchy of achievement that ensures players will not quickly lose interest. When one starts out playing the game, rewards come frequently, perhaps three or four in a matter of hours. A reward might be a special weapon, suit of armor, magic spell, or resistance to magic spells. As play continues, the rewards become fewer and farther between to the point that a player may have to play more than one hundred hours to obtain the sought-after object or battle attribute. Some players pursue the progressively less-frequent rewards by playing a moderate amount per day and having patience. A person prone to addiction, such as Darryl, responds to this situation by drastically increasing play time, often to the point of obsession. Darryl dropped out of college to pursue these online "rewards."

Not all games rely on this carrot-and-stick method.[7] Many video game addicts simply require more and more time spent playing the game to get the same level of stimulation that they previously experienced. This phenomenon is known as tolerance. Players often trick themselves into playing "just a little longer." They justify continued play with an unending sequence of irrational bargaining:

- "I'll just play for fifteen more minutes."

- "Once I get one of my characters to level twelve, I'll go to bed."

- "I know what I did wrong now. I'll just reset the level one more time and I know I'll beat it this go-around. Then I'm done."

- "If I make it to the next level, I'll feel more relaxed and I'll sleep better. Otherwise, I would just think about the game and not be able to sleep."

- "I know my fifteen minutes are up, but I'm on such a roll; I can't stop now. This is the best I've ever done."

- "I want to stop now but I can't. The members of my clan are counting on me."

- "I must have had the time wrong, because there's no way I have been playing for four hours."

Gaming and cyber addicts lose the ability to judge how long they have been playing; they experience a sort of time warp. They need more game time to get the same thrill. It's that simple. The fact that cyber addicts indulge in such deceptive self-talk shows that a part of us—the rational and healthy part—does not want to continue playing or engaging in the other cyber activity. But in spite of this desire to stop or cut back, the addict keeps playing or using, and time spent per day soon soars. Some, like me, go through binges and then stop for a while.

My friend Ken went through a period of three years of obsessive MySpace use. I saw exactly what was happening because he moved into my house for six months after his apartment building burned down. His daily pattern was to work from eight in the morning until six in the evening. He would scarf down a little food when he came home, and by seven o'clock he was on the computer. His main obsession was continually updating, changing, and editing his profile. He microfocused on the smallest details and surfed the Internet for hours looking for the right photos to augment the image he was trying to project via his profile page. "I stopped living life for three years," Ken said, "and stopped being myself. I tried to use MySpace to become this happening, edgy, artsy guy who I thought I should be." For Ken, MySpace was about projecting an image of himself and relating online to others as that image. This pursuit infused him with hope and excitement that his life could be different. "But the hope and excitement would run out," he said, "and I started having to spend more and more energy to get those feelings back. It started to feel like I was on a treadmill." Like all addicts, Ken experienced tolerance and needed to log greater amounts of time to keep his cyber-mediated delusions alive.

"JUST FIFTEEN MORE MINUTES"

Many of my best ideas have gone by the wayside because I chose to play video games. Time and time again I have kicked myself when I discovered that someone else brought to fruition an idea that I had conjured up years before. Sometimes, my video game–induced lack of productivity disgusted me, and I'd swear I would change.

For a few days, I'd play no games at all, but invariably the urge crept back in and got the better of me. "Oh, I'll just play for fifteen minutes," I would tell myself with a straight face, actually believing this self-deception. Fifteen minutes? Actually, the probability was greater that I would spend fifteen hours! "Okay, the fifteen minutes are up, but I now know what I was doing wrong in that level," I'd bargain with myself, to get over the first pangs of guilt. "I will just play for fifteen minutes more, and then I will get started on this work."

Most times, the job never got done. Eight or ten hours later, I was headlong into a video game binge yet again. I have invented elaborate stories and deceptions to cover up the truth about why I was late completing commitments, or why they did not get done at all. Like many addicts, I became a skilled liar.

Madison, a fourteen-year-old student of mine, was also gifted at deception. Her skills at tuning out with the Internet, however, were even more impressive. She kept her iPhone with her all day in school, surfing Facebook through the device and sending an average of seventy-five text messages from school on a daily basis. "I started sending a few messages on Facebook and texts a day," she said, "but I started to get really good at it. The more I did it, the more exciting it got because of the threat of getting caught." For Madison, what started as a very occasional behavior turned into an all-encompassing obsession. Her behavior was only uncovered when her mother carefully examined her cell phone bill.

"I REALLY NEED TO CUT DOWN"

"Tomorrow, I'm going to stop," Rick told himself after he peeled his body out of the computer chair at four in the morning. He resolved to get involved in a campus organization. He craved friendship. Ever since middle school, he had felt socially awkward and isolated. He had a few friends in high school, and his main contact with them was through online video games. He hoped college would be different and was sorely disappointed when the same social discontent crept back into his life.

Something about those late hours in his dorm room in front of the computer monitor caused him to reflect on the persistence of his unhappy interpersonal situation. He knew in those lucid moments that twelve to fourteen hours of World of Warcraft were a primary obstacle. He admitted that he suffered from extreme social anxiety. He said that he knew he couldn't deal with that issue unless he stopped, or at least drastically cut back on, gaming.

Rick had every intention of stopping. Sometimes, he would snap out of his post-gaming malaise with renewed commitment. "Tomorrow is the day," he declared aloud with evangelical fervor. He went to sleep feeling that he was on the verge of personal transformation. He got up and went to class, but those rumblings of social anxiety slowly percolated within him. The longer he was out in public, the more intense these feelings became. Some days, he skipped one of his later classes to get back to the safety of his room.

Once there, he didn't have much to keep himself busy. Sure, he would do some homework. Invariably, however, he convinced himself that he could log on to the game for a few minutes, just to check things out or perhaps chat with members of his guild and plan their next adventure. A few minutes was rationalized into further play as he convinced himself "how important it is that I support the team," which eventually gave way to, "I can't abandon them now." The team was, after all, the closest thing he had to a network of friends.

Rick says that he feels uncomfortable during the first hour of play, as guilt and shame gnaw at him. "After that," he said, "I merge with the game, and nothing else in the world matters."

The extreme guilt for my friend Ken was not so easily dispelled. "When I was on MySpace," Ken said, "I felt guilty the whole time and even the next day before I got on again." The guilt was not enough for him to stop. "I could see after a few months into my problem that my time on MySpace was not taking me anywhere. I wanted to meet other artists and further my dream of metal working. It just wasn't happening, but I continued for another two and a half years." Ken kept telling himself and his close friends that he wanted to spend more time on realizing his dreams, but he could not escape from being locked into MySpace.

Like many cyber addicts, Rick and Ken did not stop despite a strong will. We cyber addicts realize that we are not achieving our goals and that many aspects of our lives suffer, but we continue our destructive behavior.

THE COSTS MOUNT: CONTINUING BEHAVIOR
DESPITE NEGATIVE CONSEQUENCES

The persistence of addictive behavior despite the physical or psychological costs is an essential element of any addiction. The addict frequently denies the destructive impact of his or her behavior. When awareness of that destruction does come, often it is not enough to motivate the addict to stop. The results are shocking. Cyber junkies have played and surfed themselves into unemployment, bankruptcy, and divorce.

Mark, a friend of mine since high school, was laid off from a major company during a corporate downsizing. He received a generous severance package, which included one year's full pay. After his layoff, he found himself bored and came across a copy of Civilization IV, with an option for online gaming.

Playing Civilization IV quickly became a four- to six-hour ritual that both began and ended his day. By the time he finished his "morning" play, it was four in the afternoon—too late to search for a new job. He went on like this for months before his friends began to confront him about his self-destructive actions. He paid lip service to change, but his game time only increased. Eventually, his day became an unbroken streak of playing Civilization IV. From my own experience with the original version of this game (discussed later in this chapter), I clearly understood the degree of Mark's addiction.

Although we continued to try to intervene with Mark, he outmaneuvered us with his many rationalizations. "I worked eighty hours a week for years," he said, "and this is my time to have a little fun." We knew we could not get through to him, but we thought his obsession would peter out when he ran out of money.

Mark squirreled away money during this time because he had

no social life and did little except play the game. His frugality allowed his game binge to go on for almost another year. Eventually, however, the bills piled up, and he was forced to take time away from the game as he sought to refinance his way into financial stability. He signed an interest-only mortgage. He never bothered to get another job. The game quite simply had become his life. Now, after four years of this behavior, his condominium is in foreclosure, and he still has no job. He continues to game despite the dire financial repercussions.

The Curse of the Weather: How I Met Civilization

Through most of my college career, I was successful at staying away from games. I usually worked in addition to taking classes, so my life was quite busy. I was passionate about many of the foreign language classes I took, which helped keep my focus on my schoolwork. I was also blessed with some incredible professors who inspired me to do my best work.

It took me longer than normal to get through college because I often ran out of money and was not excited about taking on student loans. I would take a semester off, work a few jobs, and then go back. This start-and-stop pattern grew old and by 1993, my last year, I decided to incur some debt and complete my degree. During the spring term of that year, I took twelve credits on a half term which is equivalent to being a full-time student over a full-length term. The hectic nature of that term, coupled with academic fatigue that had been setting in for the previous year, burned me out. I only had enough energy to take one class during the summer term. I went from being insanely busy to not knowing what to do with myself.

A blistering week of summer heat sent me to the air-conditioned central campus computer lab at the University of Michigan. Temperatures hovered in the nineties, with high humidity. I had no idea that my attempt to escape the heat would lead me down a very dark path, nor was I aware that computer video games, as opposed to console games, had attained unique features that made me highly susceptible to their addictive influence.

I sat at my computer station next to a man named Ian, who was about my age. I knew him from a class we had together. He, too, had come to the lab to beat the heat, but he had a much more interesting distraction: Sid Meier's Civilization. I recognized my classmate right away, but he took no notice of me. I know now that his failure to recognize me was caused by the trance Civilization had induced. I distinctly remember the glaze in his eyes as he turned to see who had called his name. "What's up, dude?" he finally responded, startled. I immediately asked if something was wrong, and he casually informed me, "No, dude. I'm just playing Civ."

"Civ?" I asked, curious.

"Yeah, Civ. You'd love it because you're a history geek," he responded.

TRAVELING BACK IN TIME

During this brief exchange, it was obvious that Ian wasn't interested in talking to me; he wanted to get back to the game. To get rid of me, he took the game manual from his backpack and said I should read it. I took his suggestion, and I was hooked before I even played. The following is an excerpt from the introduction of the manual:

> Civilization casts you as the ruler of an entire civilization through many generations, from the founding of the first cities 6,000 years ago to the imminent colonization of space. It combines the forces that shaped history and the evolution of technology in a competitive environment. You have great flexibility in your plans and strategies, but to survive, you must successfully respond to the forces that historically shaped the past.[8]

Here it was, an element that my old game, Centurion, did not have: innumerable opportunities for advancement. I had control over the course of human history, and I could play as the controller of several different civilizations to exercise that control. The flexibility of decision making combined with the availability of many civilizations ensured that I would not quickly tire of the game. The game also offered five difficulty levels, from chieftain to emperor. These factors meant an exponential increase in the number of variations, thus making the game incredibly addictive.

Centurion was child's play compared to the challenges that awaited me in Civilization. As I read the manual, I began to feel excitement throughout my entire body. As I read further, the lines jumped out at me, awakening the dormant video game junkie in me:

> In Civilization, as in history, a key step and a fundamental concept is the founding and management of cities. The civilization you are about to rule begins as a prehistoric wandering tribe that has just reached that critical stage where it is capable of building cities. The first step is to build one city and from there expand. As your civilization grows, cities will spread over several islands and continents.[9]

As I read these lines even now, I am transported back to the endless possibilities that danced in my mind. "I've got to play now," the compulsive refrain went off in my head. I asked Ian where I could get the game. He told me the name of the store, but I realized with dismay that it was pretty far away, and I didn't have a car. I left the computer lab undeterred. I braved the heat, took a bus all the way to a shopping area, bought the game, and returned two hours later to find Ian still busy expanding the Hittite empire and hoping to conquer the entire world.

"TO BUILD AN EMPIRE THAT WOULD STAND THE TEST OF TIME"

For me, Civilization resulted in an extraordinary expenditure of time. I didn't own a computer, but the computer lab was always open, and eventually the Civilization addicts loaded the game onto almost every computer there. All I had to do was pop in my disk. Playing the game became the most important activity in my life, eclipsing school and social interactions, and relegating meals to a brief and barely enjoyable necessity.

Fortunately—or unfortunately, depending on one's perspective—the instructor for the political science class I was taking did not require attendance at class. There were several options for coursework, one of which was to turn in nothing except a twenty- to thirty-page research paper at the end of the course. I chose that option and did not attend class, because this allowed maximum time playing Civilization.

The computer lab attendants soon came to know me by name. Food was prohibited in the lab, but I managed to smuggle in energy bars, which became my staple. I maximized bathroom time by making sure to fill up my water bottle on the way back, and I often used these brief pauses in game play to purchase and wolf down candy bars from the vending machines.

I was not home to receive calls from friends (this was before widespread cell phone use), and I made sure that no one knew where I was spending my time. I led friends to believe that I had been researching political theory at the graduate library. Answering machine messages included invitations to go to the beach, attend parties, and go on road trips. I called no one back and did none of these previously satisfying activities.

Civilization proved a worthy foe. By the end of the summer, I had only advanced to the third level of difficulty, the prince level, and had not yet won at that level with each civilization. I estimate that in two months, I had racked up nearly five hundred hours of gaming!

This pattern continued through the subsequent fall semester, when I only enrolled in two classes because that's all I needed to graduate. My compulsive play finally paid off around Thanksgiving of that year. I beat the game on its highest difficulty level. This accomplishment left me euphoric for a week. The game had so many permutations and outcomes, however, that I was not able to stop playing it. My play time leveled off to three or four hours a day which, once I graduated, allowed me to hold down a job and meet my basic obligations.

Just as I had done during my undergraduate years, I tried to keep my gaming habit a secret. I knew that friends and family would not approve, and in my rational mind, I felt ashamed about what I was doing and guilty that I had not achieved many of my life goals.

Sleepless Nights, Bad Grades

A 2009 study showed a strong correlation between excessive daytime sleepiness and extreme Internet use in adolescents.[10] Correlations with a variety of other sleep problems were also observed. When adolescents exhibit low mental energy and are continually fatigued, Internet use should be one of the first variables examined. Sleep disturbances are often the first sign of a cyber problem. Since the brain does not function well on short sleep, problems in school, therefore, are usually not far behind.

Connor was seventeen and performing poorly in school when he came to see me in my role as an academic/learning coach. He had an IQ of 135 but suffered from ADHD. He was a math whiz who did well in calculus without really studying, but his grades in other subjects left much to be desired. He was tired all the time and frequently fell asleep during class. Connor told his mother that he had been going to bed around eleven and waking up around seven.

Eager to solve the mystery of his tiredness, Connor's mother took him to a sleep clinic. The doctors found nothing wrong. I suspected video games, but his mother did not agree. She knew he liked computer games but had never seen him playing for long periods. His sleepiness seemed to be the key to his low grades, but we did not know what was keeping him awake at night.

We were at an impasse until another boy who was a client of mine and knew Connor from school told me that Connor stayed up all night playing World of Warcraft. Connor had bragged about his online exploits on his Facebook page. When I confronted him, he admitted that this was true. It took many attempts over several weeks, however, to convince him that spending his nights on the game and not sleeping underlay his lack of academic success and constant irritability. He wanted to do well in school, cared about his grades, and he really wanted to stop gaming.

Many discussions over those several weeks culminated in Connor finally committing to face his problem. He seemed to turn over a new leaf. He brought me his copy of the game in a sort of ritual to symbolize his commitment to recovery. He actually started sleeping, and teachers began to email his mother favorable reports. It was a swift and miraculous turnaround.

He phoned me whenever he felt a relapse coming on. "Kevin, it's Connor," he'd anxiously say. "I got a new copy of the game from a friend, and I'm really close to putting it back on the computer." I talked him through it and together we figured out solutions when the cravings were intense.

I had been receiving this sort of phone call from him regularly for a couple months, and then they abruptly stopped. I naively figured the cravings had subsided. But a couple of weeks later, Connor was tired and irritable again. He would not admit to backsliding, but that same week his mother caught him playing World of Warcraft at five in the morning.

Despite Connor's desperate desire to do well in school, the need to play the game overpowered the desire for good grades. Out of desperation, his parents sent him to a therapeutic wilderness school far away from his electronic universe. Connor is thriving in that environment, but the real test will come when he returns home and has to deal with temptation.

Madison, the girl who texted and surfed Facebook while in class, initially made her way to me because of poor grades. Once her mother figured out what had been occupying her time, we all understood why she was failing most of her classes: she was texting and surfing the Web when she should have been paying attention. She had something of a schedule. During English class, she often putzed on FarmVille, and during science class, she told me that she usually caught up on Mafia Wars. In most other classes, she just texted or messaged her Facebook friends. When I asked how she settled on this schedule, she said she didn't know, but added, "I just get bored and I have to do different things different hours to keep busy." By the time I was seeing her, she had even added the game Tetris to her arsenal of distractions and was regularly staying up until three or four in the morning. Her constant access to the Internet meant that she kept busy with everything except paying attention in class and doing her school work, and her sleep deficit further impaired her ability to focus. For many teenagers, the temptations of the Internet are just too much for them to handle.

As Ken's story described previously illustrates, the sleep disturbances often associated with excessive Internet use are not confined to teenagers. Ken pulled a few all-nighters a week and often slept for twelve to thirteen hours on the weekend. "I just didn't have the focus I needed to do my metalworking," Ken said. "As I look back, I think the lack of sleep screwed up my ability to focus." Ken used to justify his weekday Internet use by telling himself that he would work on a welding project on the weekend. When the weekends would come, Ken was just not mentally and physically fit enough to follow through on plans. Like Connor's grades, Ken's dreams took a backseat to his cyber activities.

The Mental and Physical Toll

Those insane hours that I spent hunched over an inflexible computer chair during my last year at college wreaked havoc on my body. My lower back hurt. I ignored the discomfort. Soon I had pain shooting down my leg, which made walking excruciating. The next body part to suffer was my right wrist because of my constant use of the mouse. Moving my wrist at certain angles caused intense pain. I realized that game play was the culprit in all these physical complaints. My screen time, nevertheless, continued unabated—although I began to wear a wrist guard to prevent further damage. A campus physician suggested that I stop using the computer until my symptoms subsided. I ignored his advice.

Although I was a certified junkie of Civilization at this point in time, the summer of 1993, thinking about the possibility of failing my political science class caused me great anxiety. That still wasn't enough to get me to limit play time. I waited until two days before the massive research paper was due and took huge doses of caffeine pills to stay awake for two days straight to complete the paper. I cultivated a friendship with one unusually helpful librarian. She researched and found many of my sources, printed out relevant sections, and hand-delivered them to me at my cubicle. She had the makings of a great enabler. I salvaged my grade and credit for the course, but I learned next to nothing from a class that cost me approximately $900.

IN THE SHADOWS

Cyber junkies steal away to secret locations to peacefully pursue cyber pleasure away from prying eyes and inquisitive minds. We often interface with our fantasy realms in places and at times that minimize contact with the outside world. "My son is a virtual night owl," one mother told me, "and I'm not sure he ever sleeps. If I wake up at four in the morning, he's on that stupid game." A loved one gaming in the middle of the night is often the first sign of a problem.

Like most addicts, we hide our behavior. Openly displaying our tendency to excessively game or obsess over our social networking site profiles has resulted in scolding and criticism. If we live at home with our parents, we are more than happy to have our bedroom in the basement. If we live in a house with others, whether family or friends, we consider our bedroom a holy place. We deem it an extreme sign of disrespect for you to enter without permission. We do not want you in there at all. We want to be alone and uninterrupted while indulging in our obsession. Our dream is our own secluded cyber lair.

The game console and the social network interface are portals to another world. When you talk to us or the phone rings, we are forced to come back to the real world. We find that irritating. We neither desire to see your face nor hear your voice when we are in that virtual space. From our perspective, any interruption is an extreme violation. We want you to stay away.

Teens in general like to minimize parental contact. Texting is a great way to make that happen. However, there are benefits to parents using texting. First of all, it allows the parents to become more technologically savvy and enter a bit into the teen universe. Teens often respond better to texts than to a parental-voice delivered message. I had one young man whose mother complained about having to nag him to come down to dinner. Something about her nagging created resistance in this fifteen-year-old. The mother, at my suggestion, started texting him to come to dinner, and—presto!—he came down within a few minutes and no need to nag.

Yes, I do encourage parents to text with their children, but also to be vigilant about the potential for texting to be a distraction, especially in school. Watch the cell phone bills and look at the number of texts. You can even get a copy of the bill and see at what time of the day texts were sent. If a young person is texting quite a bit during the school day, it might be time to shut texting off. Most cell phone companies allow users to go online and shut off the phone and/or texting. I encourage parents to talk with a customer service representative and find out what options are available.

Teachers and school administrators should be aware that students, in spite of blatant restrictions, keep their cell phones with them all day on silent. They game, text, email, and check their Facebook page through all their classes. It is a huge problem. I work with students with ADHD and I am amazed by how often they have texted me for an answer to a test they were taking. This means that they have their cell phones with them and are able to get off text messages during teacher-supervised testing. Their cell phones are almost another appendage that many cannot live without. As smartphones get smaller with upgrades in technology, this problem is only going to get worse. Some school districts have even put cell-phone-blocking devices in their buildings to prevent use during the school day. This may be the only viable long-term solution.

SPEND TIME WITH FRIENDS OR GO ONLINE?

Those who have a cyber addict in their lives commonly feel neglected and unimportant, just as they would with any other addict. In the throes of a binge, I have turned off my phone, shut all the shades, and reacted viciously when interrupted. I did not want my union with my game or the cyber world interrupted. In those moments, I was escaping the real world, and I resented anyone who tried to bring me back. "Leave me alone!"

Most cyber addicts who come to see me, whether child or adult, experience difficulties in relationships. Sometimes those difficulties are a direct result of the compulsive cyber use, but other times existing social problems are what propel users into an alternate reality. Gamers often find themselves lost in an online fantasy world, while compulsive users of social networking sites lose themselves in online fantasy relationships. They interact through a screen for seven, eight, or even ten hours a day. Gamers join clans and guilds in games such as World of Warcraft, EverQuest, RuneScape, and Counter-Strike. They spend little time with their friends or spouses, and rush home from school or work to log on to the game so that they can support their clan. Those with social networking addictions won't be bothered to call or meet with friends, but they obsess over their MySpace and Facebook profile pages as if they were primping for a date.

The consequences for the addict, whether adolescent or adult, are severe as use spirals out of control. The addict may even fail to perform the most basic responsibilities as he or she loses a grasp on reality.

A few years back, a mother addicted to a video game left her child alone, and as a result the child died:

> An Arkansas mother was arrested after her three-year-old daughter died sweltering in a closed car while her mother played EverQuest, police told the northwest *Arkansas Morning News*. Mary Christina Cordell, 36, faces a felony charge of manslaughter in the death of her daughter. Authorities said Cordell and her boyfriend, Eric Long, 21, may have been so

fixated with the online role-playing game EverQuest that she neglected to pay adequate attention to Brianna's whereabouts on Aug. 8, the day the child died.[11]

This extreme example illustrates the power of video game addiction. The woman's need to play the game outweighed her concern for her daughter. In other cases, of course, the consequences are not deadly but are nonetheless unhealthy. "Chad used to meet with his friends at our house every Friday night to play Dungeons and Dragons," the young man's older brother informed me as we prepared for an intervention. "Yeah, they're all geeks, but they hung out and had a good time with each other." By the time I came into the picture, Chad had no human contact outside of limited interactions with family. Increasingly, he kept to himself, but he chatted daily with his online friends, his so-called "guild" members. He spoke of them as though they were his true family, although he had never met them in person.

Indeed, the social consequences of cyber addiction can be severe. Spouses of the players of EverQuest and World of Warcraft have set up email groups and Web sites to help each other deal with an addiction that has the power to destroy marriages. The news group Widows of World of Warcraft contains an endless flow of postings from emotionally unfulfilled spouses on the verge of divorce. I have read through hundreds of postings from that and other sites and have found some common themes:

- She loves that game more than life itself.

- He eats his meals at the computer almost every night.

- He talks to everybody about the game but doesn't realize that people are not interested.

- She relates to the game as if it were real, but the real people in her life are almost nonentities.

- He uses my credit card to buy [in-game] magic and weapons from other players.[12]

With all addictions, the addictive activity or substance dwarfs all other activities and the people from whom the addict once derived pleasure and sustenance. The extent to which an addict ignores loved ones is a useful measure in determining the depth of the addiction.

FINDING FRIENDS IN THE CYBER WORLD

My friend Ken has struggled his whole life in finding and keeping satisfying friendships. In high school, he was somewhat of a dilettante who moved between various social groups without becoming a full-fledged member of any of them. All of the friends he thought he had made seemed to mostly vanish after graduation. "I always felt that I was on the social periphery and longed to move toward the center," Ken said, "but I've never been able to do that." In 2003, he went to the Burning Man event in Nevada and experienced several days of what he called social bliss. At that artistic and countercultural event, he found people he deemed kindred spirits, meeting several who lived close to him. He joined the local group of "Burners" who put on events throughout the year. After a few years, however, he had that same sense of not having the satisfying friendships he longed for. It was during this period of realization that he started obsessing on his MySpace account, finding there what he thought were other like-minded folks. Once again, Ken came up short socially.

He eventually made his way into therapy and finally got to the root of his social difficulties. Ken examined the negative lessons he learned during childhood from his family relationships and saw how his fears prevented him from intimacy with others. He began to see how he unconsciously sabotaged his relationships and realized that predictable patterns operated in his life: He would get quite excited about a new friend or romantic interest, become consumed by the new connection, and then do a series of stupid things that ultimately pushed people away. Ken's MySpace time was just one in a long series of activities and behaviors that Ken engaged in instead of doing his own internal work. As I have stated several times, those of us addicted to the cyber world look to that world for what we really want in our lives, not the real world.

MISSING OUT ON SOCIAL DEVELOPMENT

Here's another example. The parents of a ten-year-old boy brought their son in to see me about a year ago. Zach was a very bright young man who had been diagnosed with ADHD. In my role as an ADHD coach, I help those with ADHD develop programs for success in school and their careers. Given that approximately one-third of individuals with ADHD will eventually have a problem with substance abuse, it should come as no surprise that many of my clients with ADHD also suffer from cyber addictions.[13]

Although Zach's parents were worried about their son's issues with school, as the initial interview continued, a more disturbing issue emerged. The boy's parents assumed that his ADHD lay behind his school troubles. He had not had any issues until the beginning of fifth grade when he started acting out with fellow classmates and started showing resistance to homework. He had been in several schoolyard scuffles, and missed assignments caused his grades to plummet.

As I dug deeper, I learned that Zach had received the Xbox 360 video game system for his most recent birthday. It became clear that he was playing the game four to five hours every day. He also spent time with a fourteen-year-old neighborhood "bad boy," going to the boy's house to watch the boy play certain games so that he could learn new tricks.

Zach decided he no longer wanted to practice karate, and he opted out of the spring soccer league. A bike he had received for Christmas went unused. He showed little interest in spending time at recess with other kids, except for one boy, who was also obsessed with video games. Zach had chosen video games over everything else.

He missed out on opportunities to learn and develop skills for relating with other human beings. In the video game universe, Zach was in complete control and did not have to negotiate or interact. If events in a game took a turn for the worse, he could simply press the reset button. He made all the decisions about how the quest or mission would proceed. No compromise was required. I am afraid that children like Zach are being deprived of the chance to learn to deal with conflict. They also do not practice the crucial give-and-take that operates in most successful relationships. When they grow up, they are at increased risk for serious interpersonal problems at work and at home.

I believe Zach's short fuse at school probably was tied to his ADHD, but playing video games only exacerbated this tendency. Teachers in school began to see emotional outbursts only after his excessive video game playing began. In the video game world, children can pursue entertainment in ways that isolate them from everyone else. Excessive video gaming definitely retards social development.

GAMING AND THE INTERNET OVERTAKE HEALTHIER ACTIVITIES

Zach's story not only illustrates the potential for video game play to damage performance at school, but reveals a cultural shift. When I was a kid, we certainly did play video games, but many parents were more vigilant about regulating game play. Our game systems were primitive compared to today's offerings, and we simply got bored after a while—even the most ardent gaming enthusiasts among us.

Parents would shoo us out of the house too. My friend Dean's mom would often scold us, saying, "You kids need to get outside." We played baseball in driveways. We walked to the park and played pickup basketball. In the fall, groups of boys and even some girls got together for games of touch football and hockey in the street. We rode our bikes everywhere.

All these activities were opportunities for socialization in addition to giving us much-needed exercise. We were forced to interact with other real, live human beings, and we had to deal with conflict. When we could not resolve our differences over whether or not someone had stepped out of bounds in a touch football game, we had a re-do. There was a shortage of kids in our neighborhood, so even if two kids didn't like each other, they were strongly encouraged to set aside their differences so that we would have enough players for a game. If one kid, like my friend Craig, stubbornly refused to come out and play, the whole gang of kids would go over to his house and beg him to come out. His mother would often step in and make him go outside because all he was doing was watching TV. Activity and adventure characterized youth culture. For a large segment of our youth population, those elements have gone missing nowadays, replaced by sitting in front of a computer screen or game console.

PSYCHOTIC BREAK

In some cases, cyber addiction can lead to complete mental breakdown. Steve, a friend since college, is one of the brightest people I have ever met. He has consistently supported me with great advice. He regularly helps his friends with their problems, yet he has never figured out how to help himself.

Steve finds the daily grind of life extremely difficult. When we were in college, he was a loner and spent most of his time in his room. In his own words, "Most people drag me down, so I prefer to avoid them." After college, he found a job as a contract computer programmer. He worked at home and did not have to interact with people, a situation for which he was most grateful.

Steve has also suffered from anxiety, a condition he medicated with marijuana. A few years ago, I learned that Steve began to augment his marijuana with a fantasy role-playing game. "With a good joint and the game," Steve told me, "I enter an altered state of consciousness and completely forget about the world." He owned two computers, one for work and one for the game. The machines sat next to each other, running simultaneously, so he was pretty much only away from the game when he slept. Steve had discovered a way to tune out the real world 95 percent of the time.

A few months ago, however, Steve completely exited reality. He called me in the middle of the night to tell me that there had been thieves and prowlers in his neighborhood. Concerned for his welfare and mindful of his paranoid nature, I agreed to let him stay at my house for a few days. I went back to bed as soon as he arrived and assumed that he had done the same.

"They're still out there!" Steve screamed, waking me out of a deep sleep at five in the morning. I bolted out of bed, certain that something had gone seriously wrong. I found Steve darting back and forth between rooms, crouching as he moved, apparently to avoid being detected by the evil doers he presumed to be outside. I could not calm him down. He insisted that we were under attack. I called his mother, who then called the police and an ambulance, and Steve was taken to a treatment center. "I am Trolor the wizard," he bellowed as the police and paramedics restrained him on the gurney. "I am the only one who can save you. If you take me away now, they will kill you all!"

Four weeks later, under medication, Steve was able to return to work, but he has never been the same. He became even more of a hermit, almost totally avoiding contact with others. His psychotic episode, I learned, followed four days of no sleep and almost uninterrupted game time. It is impossible to know to what extent his video game addiction brought on his psychosis, but I suspect that if he had been in treatment instead of the cyber world, he would be a much happier and healthier person today.

Steve's parents and friends had been after him for years to do something about his problems, but he resisted. To Steve, his reality-altering fix was the only thing that mattered.

When a cyber addiction rears its head, it is often just the tip of the iceberg. As I stated previously, people with ADHD, for example, are at a significantly increased risk for excessive Internet use and cyber addictions. I have had many folks come to see me for help with cyber addictions only to refer them for evaluation for ADHD. Many studies link problematic Internet and computer use with a variety of psychological issues, including depression, anxiety, and personality disorders.[14] The important thing to keep in mind is that cyber compulsions may not be a singular problem, but could be a co-occurring disorder.

New Games, Old Behaviors

I taught English as a Second Language in the first year after college, and in the fall of that year also started working at a school for the gifted. I liked teaching, but I did not feel passionate about it. In my fourth year as a teacher, I began to feel bored, and I was therefore more vulnerable to addictive behavior.

OUT OF THE MOUTHS OF BABES

In the fall of 1997, I was teaching middle school French and social studies along with a section of high school Spanish. I took on different subject areas to try to allay the boredom that was setting in. Three twelve-year-old boys in one of my French classes were avid gamers. They were delighted that they had a teacher with whom they could discuss gaming. It gave us a point of commonality and allowed me to connect with them.

These boys expressed great enthusiasm about a real-time strategy game called Age of Empires. A real-time strategy (RTS) game does not have the players take alternating turns, but takes place in real time. This type of game has the strategy and historical progression of Civilization, but also adds a great deal more excitement because players must respond immediately to crisis. This feature really gets the adrenaline pumping. Going from turn-based to real-time games is analogous to going from cocaine to meth.

One of the boys subscribed to a gaming magazine and extolled the virtues of the game months before it came on the market. The boys really wanted me to consider getting myself a copy. I resisted, not only because of the cost—$40 to $50—but more importantly because I was in a period in which I had committed myself to not playing anymore. I had begun to appreciate the enormous destructive impact of gaming, and I wanted to focus instead on music. I had even put together a band. Besides, my wrist still hurt. The boys insisted, despite my protests, and bought me a copy of the game for Christmas. This gift presented me with quite a quandary.

HOME ALONE!

I had my copy of Age of Empires for a few days and thought of giving it to a friend rather than risk falling again under the spell of gaming. But I got bored. Friends were busy with their families, and my roommates were out of town. I decided to open the game and look at the manual. That couldn't hurt, I thought. Once again, as with Civilization, the manual filled me with intense anticipation:

> Play one of history's twelve mightiest civilizations! Command the Greek phalanx, the world's best infantry for hundreds of years. Lead the chariots of the Hittites, or Assyrians. Build up the vast agricultural empire of Egypt, Babylon, or Sumeria. Guide the Persians from their small enclave to prominence as a world power. Guide the Shang (China), Ancient Choson (Korea), or Yamato (Japan) for control of Asia. Dominate world sea trade as the Phoenicians or Minoans.[15]

Basically, Age of Empires was Civilization times ten. I could choose from twelve civilizations and even construct Wonders of the World. My peasants could mine precious metals and collect food and wood. The range of military units was extensive, and I could tailor my army to meet my specific strategic goals and then engage in real-time combat.

As if that weren't enough, eventually I found out I could play over computer networks with other humans. Beating the game used to be a safeguard against addiction because once that happened, the thrill was gone. But Age of Empires put me in touch with addicts all over the world. Going head-to-head with a real person was fundamentally more satisfying than simply playing versus the computer until all the difficulty levels were mastered.

Mentally, I disappeared and merged into a fantasyland right in the comfort of my very own home. I felt powerful and alive. All of my senses and mental faculties were attuned to the game. All realities were shut out. Things were happening to me that I had only dreamed of. The realism of the game gripped me hard. I couldn't sleep and I did not even think about eating. The best way to describe what was going on inside me is contained frenzy. I was one with the game and didn't care about anything or anyone else.

I remember feeling guilty at about four in the morning on the first night of play. I told myself that I would not tell anyone what I had been up to. I knew they would not understand.

The first Age of Empires game was followed by a long succession of games with which I experienced similar mind-blowing, life-altering compulsion: the sequels, Age of Empires II and III, followed by games called Empire Earth, Rise of Nations, and Command & Conquer and its sequels. These are just some of many.

MARATHON CHATTING

Gaming was not my only problem. During the last few years before I got my gaming under control, I started using AOL Instant Messenger to chat online. At first, I was chatting with a few friends, but I became friends with their friends and the process exploded. Soon, I had hundreds of friends in the cyber world, many of whom lived in foreign countries. Now, this last fact is particularly important because the most enduring passion of my life is acquiring foreign languages. I presently speak six and am conversational in many more. I love language! The problem was that this love combined with the Internet proved dangerous. I often had ten to twenty different chat windows going at a time. I would be talking to people in different languages all around the world. I was checked out from reality and totally plugged into the cyber world. It was an enthralling experience that eventually filled the addictive vacuum when I stopped gaming. Although there is nothing wrong with having cyber chats with folks from all over the world, this behavior, much like gaming, became a substitute for contact with people in the real world. I remember being out running errands or working and thinking how great it would be when I got to talk to certain people online. Of course, since my focus was on these cyber contacts, I neglected the real people I saw on a daily basis. Like many addicts, I had simply traded in one addiction for a brand-new one. Specialists call this *cross-addiction*, and it's quite common. Yet I had no idea what I was doing. I started out thinking my chatting behavior was a really positive thing.

When chatting online, it is very easy to manage how we come across to people. Just like Ken obsessing over his MySpace profile details, we can take time and craft a response that is in line with the image we want to project. Instead of learning how to interact with real humans, many of us learn to be subtly deceitful, albeit unconsciously. We become adept at portraying an image, but our ability to be ourselves authentically stagnates. The trouble with chatting is that for some of us, it becomes a crutch that, while giving us a measure of interpersonal safety, limits our interpersonal development. This, of course, is the great danger of the cyber world in general: it provides those of us with unexamined issues an easy escape from reality. We can plug in and convince ourselves that we're part of a cyber world of meaning, purpose, and interpersonal satisfaction.

The Next Step

To access pornography years ago, you had to have the nerve to go to the store and ask for it. The magazines were hidden. To play video games, you had to have money to put into the machines at the arcade. To have friends and social contacts, you had to make time to physically be with people, or at least talk to them on the phone. The Internet has made all these activities excessively easy. New addictive temptations are being created every day online. People who never would have become addicts are engaging in cyber activities to great excess.

Financial ruin, alienated families, wasted potential, and perhaps a break with reality await those who do not confront their addiction. The sad fact is that once addiction firmly takes hold, it does not give up its grip easily. As discussed several times, even if video game addiction is successfully treated, the individual will be at increased risk for other addictions. One of my clients stopped his gaming habit only to become an Internet pornography junkie. After a few weeks, he spent the same amount of time on porn as he had previously on gaming.

The stories in this chapter illustrate how important it is to recognize the early warning signs of problematic cyber use before it spirals into the black hole of addiction.

You now have a working knowledge of how cyber activities progress from harmless pastimes into forces of destruction. The next few chapters provide guidance on how best to proceed once you determine that a problem exists. I discuss the pitfalls in my own recovery and offer success stories of some of the individuals I have counseled.

CHAPTER 5

climbing out of the hole

"The worst of all deceptions is self-deception."

Plato

Once a person has succumbed to the cyber world and become a full-fledged addict, the situation may seem hopeless. Temptations abound, and it's difficult to even contemplate a life that doesn't include an activity that filled so many hours and felt like a second home. Sticking to self-imposed time limits on use seems incredibly difficult; resolving to steer clear of all computers is a short-lived exercise. Settling for a life in the virtual world may seem to be the most you can hope for. I'm here to tell you this isn't true. There's more to life than the cyber universe offers. Moreover, it is possible to climb out of the hole of cyber addiction and to build a new life in the outside world. This chapter will recount my personal journey from active addiction into early recovery and discuss the struggles others addicts are likely to face during their own journeys.

Denial: It Ain't Just a River in Egypt

Any program of change or recovery starts with the realization that a problem exists. The first of the Twelve Steps of Alcoholics Anonymous is all about this very realization. It states, "We admitted we were powerless over alcohol—that our lives had become unmanageable." Once we recognize that something is wrong, we are much more likely to take action. If your doctor tells you that you have high cholesterol, you will probably make some dietary changes, or at least take a cholesterol-lowering drug. If the check engine light comes on in your car, you will take it to a mechanic to see what's wrong. When healthy people discover a problem, they try to fix it. An addicted individual, in contrast, musters all his or her power to keep awareness of the problem at bay.

An addict takes enormous pains to hide the truth. These efforts often temporarily mask the true scope of the addiction. The addict buries his or her head in the sand, oblivious that a fire rages all around. Only extreme circumstances can pull the addict out of self-deception.

Addicts need to hit bottom to realize that their lives are out of control. "Bottom" may be a divorce, financial disaster, or being kicked out of the house. For younger children, hitting bottom may mean losing all privileges (cell phone, computer, having friends over, being transported by parents), or perhaps even failing classes. Sometimes, young people wake up when they become aware of how disconnected they are from their peers. Something must happen to shock the addict into awareness of the problem. Maintaining addiction is akin to plugging holes in a dam. Hitting bottom is the awareness that the dam has burst and that you had better start swimming or you will drown.

I Can Handle Anything . . . Except the Truth

During one of my game-free phases in the late 1990s, I met with Brendan, a veteran and devotee of Alcoholics Anonymous (AA). We played chess once a week at a coffee shop and talked of many things, but addiction was by far his favorite topic. He had struggled with many addictions over the years—alcoholism, overeating, gambling, and sex—and considered himself an addiction authority. He believed that the unrecognized tragedy of addiction was that it inhibited mental development. He laid out a theory for me that, at the time, struck me as preposterous:

> An addict's emotional development ceases the moment that person turns to addiction. If you start drinking when you're

nineteen, then you're emotionally nineteen when you sober up. You've got to go through all the developmental steps that you missed.

"What absolute bullshit," I thought. I wrote off his theory as nothing more than the ramblings of an AA zealot. I believed that most of his ideas about addiction were designed to glorify recovery. He was bored, I thought, and recovery was giving his life meaning.

I was in denial about my own addiction, and I did not want anyone disturbing my carefully crafted rationalizations for my behavior. My irritation did not deter him, however, and he kept up his steady flow of Twelve Step truisms that never ceased to annoy me:

- Fake it 'til ya make it.

- To keep it, give it away.

- It's not what you know. It's what you do.

- Sick and tired of being sick and tired?

- Poor me, poor me, pour me another drink.

- Take other people's inventory until you have the courage to take your own.

- Expect nothing, appreciate everything.

Every time Brendan used one of these phrases, I wanted to punch him. One day I asked him, "Why do you always have to ruin a perfectly good chess game with your rants on addiction?"

"You have a strong reaction to this stuff," he said. "Maybe you're running from something."

Angry, I replied, "You're a born-again addict, and I don't need to be saved, so leave me alone!" In spite of my irritation, I kept coming back to the coffee shop for our weekly chess game.

Twelve Step Junkie?

Brendan lived the AA lifestyle. Every other sentence out of his mouth could be traced to his devotion to the Twelve Steps. "Recovery from addiction is a spiritual process," he pontificated from his chair at the coffee shop. Like many recovering addicts, he smoked incessantly and drank one cup of coffee after another. His sermon sanctimoniously continued, "We have to let go and let God." As he spoke, he stretched out his arms and moved them up and down, mimicking a scale, hoping to get his listeners to weigh the seriousness of his words.

On one occasion, he planted himself at my table while I was in the middle of a chess game and started in, "We live in an addictive world, and alcohol and drugs are the least of our worries."

I bristled at his unsolicited sermon, especially when he followed up his proclamation by suggesting that I might have a problem with gaming. I was surprised that he knew about my binges. Unbeknownst to me, my friend Doug, who was the only person who knew about my gaming problem, had told Brendan stories of my game binging. Brendan's assertion that I had a video gaming problem left me feeling violated. I hadn't asked for his advice, and I certainly didn't want any help from him. I went through the roof when I next saw Doug. "How could you tell my personal business to that AA freak?" I demanded. I felt that Doug had betrayed me.

You Can Lead a Horse to Water

"I just wanted to help," Doug defended himself. "You always say that you want to stop playing video games," he gingerly continued, hoping to ride out my rage until he could talk sense into me.

I wanted nothing to do with Brendan and told Doug that both of them were on my "shit list." I didn't talk to either of them for a few weeks and avoided the coffee shop. I hadn't been that angry since my teen years when I confronted my alcoholic stepfather about the years of torment he had put our family through.

But the incident at the coffee shop awoke something in me. I couldn't stop thinking about what Brendan had said, nor could I rid myself of the disgust that nibbled at me. The intensity of my anger surprised me. I know now that addicts in denial often lash out at anyone who suggests there is anything wrong. Nobody was going to tell me I had a problem!

A few weeks later, I had calmed down. I got up the nerve to talk to Brendan, certain that I could dissuade him from his belief that I had a problem. The veils of secrecy and denial that surrounded my addiction had been ripped open, and I meant to sew them back together.

I sought out Brendan and started a carefully worded speech that I had prepared: "I thought about what you said, and I don't think I have a problem."

He did not argue. He actually congratulated me for not having a problem. But I wanted to argue! I had carefully planned my answers to every possible argument he might make. He patiently told me, "You're the only one who can really decide if you have a problem." He sounded like he had no stake in the situation. "If you have things under control, more power to you." His disengaging and disinterested responses disarmed me. I was sporting for a fight, but he would not engage.

As I drove home, I thought, "Maybe I do have a problem." Somehow, his adept handling of the situation opened me up to a new possibility—that there might actually be something wrong. I started going to the coffee shop again, and slowly, I shared details of my life with him.

He got me to admit, after many conversations over several months, that I had a problem. He suggested that I had been angry about things that had nothing to do with him or Doug. He said, "Most of us keep our addictions alive to avoid our unpleasant emotions, like anger, and I suspect that you're avoiding a lot of your emotional stuff through video games." I knew he was right, but I was not yet willing to open up completely. "You got mad," he said, "because Doug and I lifted the blanket of denial. But," he continued, "we should have gone about that a lot differently.

I'm sorry if I came on too strong." His willingness to admit his mistakes made me trust him.

Brendan possessed rare intuition, garnered, no doubt, from personal experience. He demonstrated this ability when he nonchalantly asked me, "How many goals in your life have you not achieved because of playing too many video games?" I didn't answer him, but this question was the one I needed to hear. It hit a nerve, though I did not yet understand why.

Feeling Is Painful

I had no peace of mind from that point on. I asked myself again and again, "What am I trying to avoid? What am I hiding from?" I questioned my behavior and motives. The answers did not come quickly. I started to review the events that led me to compulsive gaming. I attained a tenuous understanding of my behavior as I discovered the triggers to my addictive binges.

I saw how my video game binges often started during particularly stressful times or when I was bored or lonely. As I slowed down and thought through the steps that led to my binges, I began to understand: avoidance was the common denominator. I played games to avoid unpleasant emotions or uncomfortable thoughts. I played games because I felt helpless. I played because I couldn't change. I knew I wanted more out of life. I had known that for a long time. The tools to change had eluded me, however. Video games made me powerful in the face of my perceived weakness and isolation. They allowed me to anchor myself to something external when, inside, I felt disconnected. Games allowed me to be the master, the ruler, even the god of an alternate universe. I had complete control. Ironically, it was that complete control that had caused chaos in my real life.

Escaping the Pain

I came to believe that my cravings for control related to how helpless I had felt when I was growing up. I had lived in a dysfunctional environment that I could not change. In my adult life, I re-created this situation repeatedly. I never knew what it felt like to have power over my life, even when, as an adult, I did possess such power.

A large part of my work in accepting the reality of my cyber addiction was simply to become conscious of this power so that in the moments when the cravings came, I realized I had the power to make a choice. I had lived most of my life as a victim, complaining about all the raw deals that were dealt to me. Instead of accepting that my choices created my life, I blamed other people and situations that were beyond my control.

I temporarily escaped responsibility when I entered the cyber world because video gaming shut down my mind to everything else. The same temporary end was achieved later through excessive Facebook and online chatting. I didn't have to think or feel anything real. So much stimulation came at me that there was no opportunity for unpleasantness to worm its way through. The cyber world let me temporarily escape the anxiety that was following me through life.

Members of Adult Children of Alcoholics groups talk about an ever-present anxiety that comes from growing up with the unpredictability of an alcoholic household. When we grow up with an alcoholic, we feel helpless to change our situation, but we still long for stability. We become accustomed to worry and insecurity and accept them as normal.

John Bradshaw, noted author and addiction specialist, says that one of the most insidious aspects of growing up with an alcoholic is the no talk rule.[1] Fear keeps family members from bringing up the issue with each other, and shame ensures that few outside of the family ever find out. We kept our feelings inside and tried to appear to the rest of the world as a normal family.

Many of us become people pleasers, seeking stability in the family by making others happy and by trying to fix their problems before they get out of control. We take this behavior into our adult lives, but ultimately, since it derives from a conflict-laden childhood, it does not leave us feeling fulfilled. Because we do not find the emotional sustenance we need from our families, we seek substitutes, a tendency that sets us up for addiction.

My avoidance patterns go back to my late childhood. In an effort to avoid the stress of living with an alcoholic stepfather, I concentrated on my studies to avoid feelings that were hard for me to bear. As I hunkered down into the rhythms of high school, I disengaged not only from my stepfather, but from most of my friends as well. My emotions were in such disarray that I felt ill-equipped to deal with the intricacies of teenage interaction.

I stopped growing as a person though, as I increasingly became an automaton of academic achievement. My social skills stagnated. I cared more about my grades than I did about having friends. When people tried to befriend me, it frightened me to have anyone too close. I kept my distance, emotionally. I was in the top of my class academically, but in the bottom socially.

My antisocial behavior continued as my addictive energies turned from school to video games, and later to online social networking and chatting. I developed an addiction that kept me isolated from people. As I look back to both high school and college, I see that I had not developed the ability to read social cues. I neither understood how to maintain friendships, nor did I have a clue about how to help them grow. Just as Brendan had said, my addiction had caused me to miss out on developmental steps that I needed. When I finally did start the process of recovery from my cyber addiction, it was a long while before I could successfully navigate through friendships and relationships.

RON'S STORY: IT'S NOT DENIAL; "I JUST WANT TO BE THE BEST"

Again, no solutions are possible without the addict's admission that something is wrong. This truth was reinforced to me during my research phase of writing this book. I was playing a game called Counter-Strike to learn more about first-person shooter games when I met Ron, a man who saw nothing

continues

wrong with putting his entire life on hold for a video game. Thankfully, Counter-Strike turned out not to be my cup of tea, but Ron thought the game was going to make him rich.

Ron and I became part of the same clan in Counter-Strike. He lived close to me, and when I told him I was writing a book about video games, he was thrilled to be interviewed. This twenty-seven-year-old had worked as a customer service manager an average of seventy hours a week for five years. He had saved his money and built up an impressive 401(k) account.

Six months before we met, he had cashed it in and quit his job so that he could pursue Counter-Strike full-time. When I suggested that he suffered from an addiction, he laughed and said, "I just want to be the best in the game." He had heard of a guy who made his living from participating in video game tournaments and decided that was the life he wanted. "I think there's a good chance I could go pro," he told me, with the naïveté of a ten-year-old who thinks he'll grow up to be an NFL quarterback.

Ron's life revolves around the game, and he doesn't even think he has problem. In self-help circles, folks often say, "Denial ain't just a river in Egypt." Ron believed he was going to make hundreds of thousands of dollars in video game tournaments, and maybe even get some endorsements from gaming companies. No information to the contrary could dent his irrational dreams.

Rationalization Gives Way to Recovery

I created elaborate rationalizations to keep myself in denial. Rather than admit to the enormous waste of my talents, I convinced myself that my unbelievably excessive online chatting was helping me forge a vast international network of friends, people whom I could visit and with whom I was creating long-lasting bonds of friendship. As far as gaming, I told myself that it served some higher purpose. "I'm delving into history," I told myself in the middle of a Gettysburg! binge. "I am getting into the minds of J. E. B. Stuart and Robert E. Lee," I would say to pump up myself to counteract my feelings of guilt. I relied heavily on my imagination to perpetuate my dance of self-delusion. Eventually, I ran out of tricks. It simply became impossible to deceive myself. I started to see that something was wrong, but I didn't know what to do about it.

The coffee shop incident with Brendan marked a major turning point. No one had ever challenged my behavior, primarily because I had kept it hidden. No matter how determined I was to ignore what Brendan had said to me, he ruined my video game bliss forever. He suggested I had a problem, and something inside of me believed him. My rationalizations and self-deceptions provided me with less and less reassurance. In the middle of a video game, I would remember things he had said. These thoughts interrupted my once happy gaming sessions. I became so frustrated that I would rip out the power cord and storm off on a bike ride to blow off steam. Brendan planted a seed, and boy, did it grow!

Ultimately, Brendan and my friend Doug helped me to see that video game addiction controlled my life. I vacillated between gratitude for their concern and anger that they would not leave me alone. I was still gaming, but I was willing to talk about it and admit to some of its destructive effects.

I had begun to agonize about how few of my goals I had accomplished. Brendan and Doug latched onto that realization like pit bulls and never let go. I still don't know why they even bothered, but I am grateful that they did. I see their work with me as a model for anyone who has an addict in his or her life who needs help.

Sharing versus Lecture

Although the initial discussions about my addiction were confrontational, Doug and Brendan took a slow and methodical approach to helping me into recovery. They casually invited me into discussions rather than bullying me into confrontation. They were the only two people to whom I entrusted the full scope of my video game compulsion. I grew to confide in them, especially Brendan. Doug got the ball rolling, but Brendan's wisdom and experience with addictions were crucial to my decision to dive into recovery.

Brendan helped ignite my desire to stop simply by getting me to talk about my addiction. Every time I told him what seemed a particularly shameful episode of video game madness, Brendan managed to bring up a parallel example from his drinking days. He did not share these incidents in a righteous, "I once was lost but now I'm found" manner, like so many of the recovering addicts I have encountered.

"I feel worthless and pathetic when I succumb to video games," I cautiously whispered to Brendan. He said, "I felt ashamed of my drinking, so I would drink more, and then I would feel more ashamed." Then for a while he said nothing, allowing space and time for me to respond. The pauses and empty space became some of my most valuable moments with Brendan, because I got the sense that he had no agenda and was not judging me. I had hidden my addiction from everyone. My talks with Brendan were the times that I could display all aspects of myself, even the undesirable and shameful ones.

As he recounted his sordid history of lost jobs, relationships, and months-long binges, he indirectly gave me permission to come clean. I began to feel compassion for him, and soon I felt connected to a man who I had once despised. I started to see myself in him and began to see my story in the same terms that he saw his own. Thanks to his openness, I came to uncover the deeper roots of my problem.

It Gets Worse Before It Gets Better

As I revealed more of my cyber behaviors to Brendan, he became convinced that I was dealing with an actual addiction. He thought that the Twelve Steps of recovery were the path of choice. I had, without knowing it, been working on Step One: I knew that I was powerless over the cyber world. It held me in a seemingly magical spell. I knew that I had lost the ability to choose. I had no willpower, and the second I began to play one of my games, or started chatting online, I fell into an "abyss of bliss" that I found incredibly difficult to climb out of.

While on a binge, I thought of little else besides my game or my multiple chatting windows open on the computer screen. Although I was able to fulfill the basic responsibilities of home and job, my heart was in the game. When I exited a binge, I was overwhelmed by shame and guilt; I was horrified in those post-binge periods by thoughts of how much of my life I had just wasted and how few of my goals I had worked toward.

Ironically, the emotions I felt after a binge often thrust me into more excessive cyber behaviors because I could not tolerate the discomfort that had arisen as a result of the first binge. This, of course, touches on the escapism facet of my addiction. I tried to soothe my emotions through my cyber behaviors and never really grew up. Talking with Brendan helped me to finally admit this unpleasant truth. As I confided in him how awful I felt most of the time, he responded, characteristically, with one of his Twelve Step maxims: "It has to get worse before it can get better."

Nothing to Show for My Life

Brendan struck a chord when he asked me if gaming prevented me from accomplishing my goals, which all related to creative pursuits that I had never fully engaged (music, comedy, and writing). I also struggled in romantic relationships, sometimes preferring the cyber world to doing the things that would have helped me grow and develop with significant others.

I had always wanted to have a rock band. I never got past fantasizing about singing and playing for my adoring fans. I had been told how naturally funny I was, so I thought about pursuing stand-up comedy. I couldn't watch Comedy Central, nor could I stomach MTV. I found it unbearable to see others doing things I knew I could do but had taken no steps to bring to fruition.

I believed that I had three books in my head and that I just needed to spend time at my computer for the words to flow. I would sit down and start to write, but inevitably writer's block gripped me. My remedy was to unplug from the writing process and plug into a computer game for "just a few minutes." Those minutes, of course, turned into hours, days, or months. I experienced ever-increasing disappointment at how my life had turned out.

Hitting Bottom: Dreams Unfulfilled

The pain of unrealized dreams pushed at me. I had had enough. From TV, magazines, radio, and billboards, images of other people realizing their dreams bombarded me. I became jealous of others because I was sure that they all lived creative and meaningful lives. I knew I had a lot of talent, but I had nothing to show for it. I felt as though I were on the outside watching everyone else live life. I didn't like myself very much.

One day I sought out Brendan at the coffee shop to vow, "I am never playing a game again." He nodded approvingly but said nothing to me, resuming his conversation with another cafe rat (as we regulars were known). I sat sipping my tea and reading a magazine, perplexed that Brendan had made no attempt to interact with me. After letting me stew for ten minutes or so, he asked, "Do you need any support around this?"

Surprised at the question, I retorted, "Why would I need support?" Brendan explained how difficult a cold-turkey approach to ending addictive behavior could be. He related story after story of friends who had tried it and failed. Annoyed at his unceasing flow of AA failure stories, I said, "I hear what you're saying, but I'm pumped up about stopping."

He replied, "The excitement is going to end, and you will need support." He seemed irritated at my insistence on going it alone.

On My Own

I remember shortly thereafter watching a TV commercial for one of the prescription "miracle drugs" on the market. I felt like the smiling, enthusiastic, invigorated people that I saw. Their lives had been transformed by the drug. I identified with those invigorated former arthritis sufferers because I had attained what seemed to me a new lease on life. I had exited a fog, and everything around me seemed alive and pulsating. Food tasted better. I enjoyed my friends for the first time in years. I made plans to go on a canoe and camping trip, and I put an ad in a local artists' newspaper hoping to find musicians to start a band. Yes, I finally had taken a step toward fulfilling one of my dreams.

I thought about the endless possibilities for success and fulfillment. I had seen the light. My first thought was to try to help others. I wanted to offer support to struggling gaming addicts, but I didn't think I needed any myself. I felt so full and empowered, and I wanted to share that feeling. I believed that I could help other addicts transform their lives just like I had transformed my own. Euphoria swept me off my feet in those first few weeks. I thought I could accomplish anything with a simple wave of my hand.

Evangelical Recovering Addict

"How can I help people stop?" I asked myself. "If I approach them in the right way, they will want to stop," I thought, drawing on my experiences with Brendan. Acquaintances in my early years had suggested that I would make a good preacher. Well, in my antigaming, fire and brimstone fervor, I proved them correct.

A few days into my decision to stop gaming, I was spending as much time in antigaming efforts as I had in play. I lay in ambush in chat rooms until three in the morning. I emailed gaming friends telling them how great my life was since I had stopped. I hoped to be a beacon for recovery, and I devoted myself completely to spreading the word to the gaming world.

I neglected to say that I was less than a week into my own recovery. "You don't know what you're missing," I repeated enthusiastically to hundreds of gamers. I tried to entice them by giving details of the things I was "accomplishing," hoping to whet their appetites for recovery, desperate to hit a chord with them as Brendan had done with me. "I'm living real life, dude, and I have my own rock band," I wrote in an online gaming forum, certain that the rock band angle would get my foot in the door with younger gamers. I did not provide the details, however, failing to tell them that I was the only member of the band. I was willing to say anything that might open them to new possibilities.

I first tried to empathize with other gamers as Brendan had done with me. "I understand. I've been there." I wrote those lines thousands of times in many gaming chat rooms. Most gamers never even responded.

It was like trying to hold an AA meeting at a bar. I kept at it for weeks. I called gaming friends constantly and tried to arrange to meet with them. I had no takers. "I can't chat now. I'm about to get into a game, dude," said one gaming acquaintance, dismissively. "Dude, my mom begs me every day to stop gaming," another annoyed gaming friend told me. "How are you different from her?" That question stung. I not only failed to get gamers to see the light, but now I was reduced to the level of a nagging mother.

My only success was a mother who had a teenage son whom she believed was addicted to Command & Conquer. She hung out in the game forums hoping to find solutions to her son's addiction. When she found me, she convinced herself that I was the answer to her prayers.

I made the mistake of giving her my cell phone number, and she called me several times a day, asking me to pray for her son. The mother needed Co-Dependents Anonymous because she refused to restrict her fourteen-year-old son's gaming time. She made no effort to curtail any of the boy's privileges. She thought that our combined prayers could bring about a miracle. I asked her to stop calling me, and in my last conversation with her I conveyed a piece of Twelve Step wisdom: "God helps those who help themselves." How proud I was as I delivered that zinger. I also realized that I needed to follow my own advice. I needed to help myself by reaching out for support.

I Lost That Loving Feeling

I called Brendan and asked if we could meet at the coffee shop. I finally got up the courage to eat my pride. "Are you depressed yet?" Brendan wanted to know. "Yes, I am," I replied, "and I have been gaming nonstop for the last twenty-six hours."

We met an hour later, and Brendan confirmed that he had been waiting for my relapse. "I was feeling great and doing so well," I said. "I just don't know what happened."

"What happened," Brendan said, "is that this is extremely hard work, and I don't know anyone who's been able to do it alone."

Still not understanding what had gone wrong, I responded, "But I was so excited, and I thought I could help people."

"Help people?" he asked. He launched into one of his sermons. It was one I had needed to hear:

> How can you help others when you don't even know how to help yourself? You got all wound up thinking that you were going to be the messiah to video gamers. You did do something right though. You learned a lesson about dealing with addicts: you can't help them unless they want to help themselves. And you can't deal with your problems by trying to help others deal with theirs. You have to do your work first, and then possibly you can become the savior to the world of video game junkies. When you're a few steps down the path, then maybe you can share with other people how you got there.

He was right. The only thing between me and my addiction was my narcissistic zeal that I had the truth and other people didn't. I was trying to make up for all my feelings of worthlessness by aggrandizing myself as the all-knowing, all-powerful recovering video game junkie. While it's true that many recovery programs, especially Twelve Step programs, advocate helping others as part of long-term recovery, I was just starting out and was not in a position to be offering advice. My eagerness to help others served only to keep the focus off of the work that I needed to do. Later on, once I had made it through the first year, I was able to start helping others, a fact which helped confirm me in my decision to cultivate a healthy relationship with computers and stay away from the addictive behavior that had stunted my personal and professional growth for so many years. In Twelve Step recovery programs, helping others is an instrumental part of maintaining long-term recovery, but before I could assist anyone else, I had to establish a solid support network and delve deeply into my own issues. Helping others early on in my recovery was something I had used to avoid my issues. A Twelve Step maxim captures this situation well: "Take other people's inventories until you have the courage to take your own."

The Cravings! The Cravings!

Once I gave up the delusions of grandeur, the day-to-day grind of recovery weighed heavily. Video game cravings gripped me. I woke up in the morning thinking of a game. A persistent inner voice muttered the same seemingly reasonable notion: "A little game time can't hurt you, can it?"

The more successful I became at using positive pursuits to distract myself from gaming, the louder and more urgent the inner voice grew. "Play just a little bit and it will help relax you and then make you more creative," the voice said. The voice had a life of its own, almost as if it were an entity separate from me. "You're strong enough now," the voice coaxed, "you can play for a bit and then stop." I had never understood what it meant to battle an inner demon until I struggled with this voice.

Sometimes, I woke up in the middle of the night, and the first thought I had was to play a game. "Play for a few minutes and then you'll sleep better," said the ever-vigilant voice. I wanted the voice to stop. I raged at myself for my inability to ease my mind. I slapped my head repeatedly, hoping to destroy the unwanted messages. Sometimes I banged my head against the wall, where indentations remain, reminding me of these maddening episodes. A force other than reason operated in me, and I had no clue how to squelch it. I felt that terrorists had taken over a part of my brain. They refused to let go and were not open to negotiation.

The terrorist metaphor is not an exaggeration. In spite of a solid commitment to stay off of games, the cravings continued. No reasoning or logic lessened the hold the cravings had on me. I hated them! Every morning I awoke only to renew the struggle. Months passed, but the cravings would still creep up and grab me, especially in times of stress. I picked up other compulsive behaviors to try to stave off video games.

I indulged obsessively in exercise in an effort, ironically, to gain some balance in my life. I went to the gym seven days a week, sometimes twice a day. I lifted weights, worked on my abs, and did an hour of cardio training five days a week.

After a few months, I cut back, only to launch into an obsession with becoming a contestant on the TV game show *Jeopardy!* I bought twenty-eight books on trivia and loaded my iPod with *The History of World Literature* and *Great Scientific Ideas That Changed the World.* Every minute I was not working, I was studying for *Jeopardy!* I had friends, family, and random folks at a breakfast coffee shop constantly quiz me. After an audition, I was elated for a few weeks, but I became depressed when they did not call me. They have yet to ask me to be on the show.

I Just Needed Some Friends

I alienated several friends in my *Jeopardy!* frenzy. I felt a serious lack of social outlets in my life after this, which is what sent me into online chatting. It all started out because one acquaintance of mine from high school and I kept in touch via AOL Instant Messenger (AIM). He had a few friends in Europe with whom he was keeping in touch. One of his friends was on an exchange program in Spain and needed help with some translation. She and I started chatting on AIM and through her, my friends' list started to balloon. I found the whole thing incredibly engaging and started to go into some of the many chat rooms as well, adding more people to my list. Within a few months, I was spending almost as much time chatting as I had in gaming, and a disturbing feature emerged: I was losing sleep to online chatting, putting my ability to function in my career in jeopardy. Here was another activity that started as an innocuous distraction but had come to consume me yet again. True, I had stayed away from video games, but my eight-hour-a-night chatting habit told me that I had to take my recovery to a different level. Once again, Brendan's support was crucial in my efforts to drastically cut down on chatting.

The Next Step

After wasting years of my life playing video games and chatting online compulsively, I had finally turned a corner. It didn't happen all at once and the difference between quitting and staying quit was immense. Still, I had gotten my life back. The next chapter describes how I found a way to fill the numerous hours that cyber addiction once consumed. I realized that without some new healthy activities that I enjoyed, I would probably end up interminably planted in front of a computer screen in short order.

CHAPTER 6

the journey of recovery continues

"A journey is a person in itself; no two are alike. And all plans, safeguards, policing, and coercion are fruitless. We find after years of struggle that we do not take a trip; a trip takes us."
John Steinbeck

Recovery is a journey without a definite end. Particularly with substance abuse addictions, recovering addicts often say they are in recovery their entire lives—that they are never recovered. This speaks to the challenges we face and the continual risk of slipping back into addictive behavior. It's true that we can never let our guard down entirely. While that may be upsetting to people who are new to recovery, those of us who have been at it for a while know that recovery is not a sentence we have to endure. Rather, recovery is a new start at life that promises fulfillment at a level we never could have achieved through addiction. This chapter outlines the arduous journey I made from early recovery to find the peace and contentment of a new life without the stranglehold of addiction. Many other stories are shared here as well, to illustrate the individual course of this journey.

Successful Recovery: Whatever Works

Addicts are individuals, and what works for one may not work for another. My personal journey was largely punctuated by trial and error. Once I had committed to getting on with my life, I was willing to try just about anything I thought might help.

I am careful not to steer my clients toward methods that worked for me, but rather to challenge them to come up with their own steps to recovery. Some successful recovering addicts I have worked with have found support close to home, while others have needed inpatient treatment. One young man joined the Army and was sent to Iraq before he unlocked his door to recovery.

Every successful recovery contains some basic ingredients. All recovering addicts need plenty of support. They need people on call who can talk them through cravings and the issues that may send them back into a binge.

Joining a recovery group also may help. Hearing about other people's successes and failures encourages and guides us on our own journeys. Reaching out for support is the firewall that can prevent us from falling off the path. A Twelve Step saying holds that, "the most important word in the Steps is the first one: *we*."

A successful recovery from cyber addiction also means finding productive pursuits to fill the time once spent in front of the computer screen. Once we stop our compulsive behavior, we don't know what to do with ourselves. We once filled six, eight, or ten hours a day with cyber behaviors. We have to find other activities that engage and fulfill us. Otherwise, we will be bored and alone and more prone to indulge our addiction. We must look for hobbies, volunteer opportunities, and other activities that allow us to be with other people. It is when we are home alone that we are most vulnerable to relapse.

Finding Support: A Wise Elder

In the early stages of my recovery, I went to the coffee shop every day. These daily trips got me out of the house, put me in contact with other people, and kept me away from games.

Through Brendan, who was often there, I met Bill, a wild-eyed octogenarian with a mane of thick and unkempt silver hair. His piercing eyes spoke volumes even as he, characteristically, kept silent. He wore Birkenstock sandals and loose-fitting, colorful clothes. He mostly sat in a corner by himself reading poetry.

I had dismissed him as a New Age kook, but I soon found that my judgment about him was wrong. I learned that he was a retired automotive executive who had done extensive recovery work. He had abused alcohol and gambling to cope with seventy-hour work weeks and back-biting colleagues. When I met him, he had been sober for more than twenty years.

Bill told me he owed the success of his recovery to quieting his nagging inner voices. "You have to find a place within," he said, "where you can anchor yourself and simply observe what goes on in your mind." Bill had chosen meditation as his anchor. He was careful, however, to make no suggestions that I follow his example. "You have to find your own path," he said, "because recovery is both personal and spiritual work."

Bill's words still resonate for me. He is the wise grandfather I never had. I took his suggestions to heart and embarked on a wild ride.

STUMBLING TOWARD THE PATH

I picked up a weekly self-help newspaper at the coffee shop, looking for a magic bullet of spiritual transformation. In that week's issue, I learned that a swami from India was in town to initiate followers. The ad read, "Quiet Your Mind and God Will Speak." It sounded like exactly what I needed.

I paid several hundred dollars for the privilege of being initiated into the ancient yogic discipline of Swami-ji. I sat silently on a round meditation cushion in a secluded room of the large suburban house where Swami-ji was teaching. After about a half hour, Swami-ji's assistant beckoned me by banging two wooden blocks together. I followed him into the next room, where I found the spiritual teacher with flowing black hair robed in orange.

I struggled to follow his heavily accented, sing-song English. He instructed me to cover my eyes with my index fingers and simultaneously insert my thumbs into my ears. "This technique," he said, "allows you to shut out the noise of the world and to focus on the sound and light of God." Then, I was to shift my attention at regular intervals from one *chakra*—or energy point in the body—to another.

As I moved my attention up and down the chakras and blocked out all visual and auditory stimuli, I was gripped by the feeling that I had just wasted an awful lot of money. I became irritated and remember thinking, "If anger were enlightenment, I'd be the Buddha."

In spite of my strong, negative reactions, I was determined to get my money's worth. I sat cross-legged on my meditation cushion in front of the home altar that I had constructed according to Swami-ji's specifications. Every day for a month, I covered my eyes and ears for fifteen minutes and listened for the sound of God while waiting for his light. I shifted my attention up and down the seven chakras until I thought my head would explode. Swami-ji's yoga helped me develop self-discipline because I stuck with it, which was a very new behavior for me. It did not, however, give me the peace of mind I was looking for. I was ready to try a different path.

I focused on personal growth and transformation with the same vigor and obsession I had with video games and the Internet. I stuck it out through ten days of a silent meditation retreat, which featured an old Buddhist monk who used a ceremonial stick to hit participants across their backs if he suspected that their attention was wandering. I still can't believe I made it for ten days without talking. It was brutal!

Over the years I tried three different meditation techniques and found all of them encumbered by unnecessary complexity. I did one-on-one therapy with four different therapists, group therapy with three different groups, and participated in Native American rituals with four different tribes.

For my vision quest, I spent three days in the desert with only a jug of water. Calorie deprivation and the heat of the desert led to hallucinations which, according to the medicine man, contained messages and insights from the spirit world. I couldn't stop thinking that the desert teemed with tarantulas and scorpions. Every sound renewed the fear that something was about to sting, bite, or eat me. Among the tribes farther to the North, the sweat lodge is the preferred method of spiritual purification. Much like the Scientologists with their emphasis on the sauna to clear the soul, the sweat lodge involves heating rocks and pouring water over them to create an almost unbearably hot chamber of so-called spiritual renewal. It is believed that participants get close to the ground— Mother Earth—and sweat out their spiritual and psychological impurities, thus opening them to a new way of being. The experience just made me feel sick.

A friend and I trekked to the high Andes in Peru to meet with native shamans. They are fond of herbal preparations to elicit spiritual awakening. I still do not know exactly what they gave me, but I will never forget the three days of crippling diarrhea that followed my drinking the potion. The shaman reassured me, "Kevin, the plant is cleansing you to make way for new life." That experience cost me only $3,200.

Although I didn't find the magic solution I was seeking, all these methods and practices did have value for me. I slowly learned how to be silent. I was exposed to seekers, people who believed that personal transformation was possible. Those people helped me persevere. Most of them seemed to be getting something out of these programs, spiritual practices, and disciplines. I continued trying new approaches because I reasoned that I had just not found the right one.

After the Peru trip in 2003, though, I was especially demoralized. I had spent what seemed a small fortune and wasted years trying to find the elusive answer to my discontent. I certainly had gleaned bits of insight along the way, but I never discovered the earth-shattering self-awareness I craved. I wanted to discover an ancient wisdom that would open my sky and ignite a fire within me. Up through the end of 2003, I repeatedly relapsed into bouts of gaming binges.

Like many addicts, the routines of life wear me down, so I was searching the spiritual realm for something exciting and extraordinary that would inject meaning into my life. I wanted a magical life, similar to the one I had lived in the cyber world. As I came to realize that magic was not going to happen, I grew depressed. I not only became disillusioned about recovery, but I was disgusted, feeling that I had wasted even more of my life. Luckily, Bill was still hanging out at the coffee shop. I sought his counsel.

BACK TO THE BASICS

"Gratitude is not only the greatest of virtues,
but the parent of all others."
—Cicero

"I think it's a losing battle," I told Bill as we sat in the coffee shop. "You told me that I had to find an anchor, but I still feel like a ship lost at sea." I rattled off a litany of my dissatisfactions with life.

Bill listened intently and, after about thirty minutes, said, "I know you're not a drinker, but I think there's something you need to hear," he said. "Poor me, poor me, pour me another drink."

I remembered that Brendan had often uttered the same line, but it wasn't until Bill used it on me that I fully understood its meaning. "Self-pity is the surest road to relapse," Bill said.

As an experiment, Bill asked me to keep a notebook next to my bed. First thing in the morning and before going to bed, I was to write down a "gratitude list" of at least ten things for which I was grateful. He told me that there were many aspects of life that we all take for granted, and that most of us have a tendency to focus on the negatives and obsess over what we do not have. "Whatever you choose to focus on," Bill told me, "that's what you will get out of life. If you let your mind become overrun with things you are unhappy about, those things are what you end up getting."

I could not imagine that this simplistic method would do anything to lift my spirits. I had been to the high Andes and to arid deserts, and I had apprenticed under shamans and holy men, but nothing had helped. I was disappointed that this list idea was the only solution Bill could suggest. I left the coffee shop more depressed than ever.

I had so much respect for Bill, though, that I did what he asked. I figured I might have a few things to write down each day. Bill asked me to spend at least five minutes each time I opened the notebook so that "gratitude could percolate." On the first day, I wrote:

1. My health
2. I have a job I do not hate
3. Barb
4. Palmer
5. My friend Brendan
6. I speak many languages
7. Doug
8. My cat, Lulu
9. I have a great house
10. I live in a great neighborhood
11. I live in a time when doctors can cure most infectious diseases
12. Working in the afternoon so I don't have to wake up early
13. I am able to go to Monty's every day, drink coffee, and hang out
14. I was lucky to get a great education
15. My mom always supported my dreams
16. I have had great mentors in my life
17. My family
18. I play the guitar
19. I am funny
20. I have a good car

21. My mom is in good health
22. Emily
23. Languages come easily to me
24. I am not poor
25. I have traveled around the world
26. I live in a relatively free country
27. I am not a poor farmer living in the Third World
28. I was not around when Mt. Vesuvius erupted
29. Chocolate
30. I grew up in an open-minded family
31. The stock market hasn't crashed in over seventy years
32. Hitler is dead
33. The killer bees never made it up to Michigan

The first items came slowly, but after a couple minutes, my gratitude exploded! I had fun with the exercise, and each day, the list grew longer. And something amazing happened: I found that I was grateful through most of the day. Depression and gratitude could not coexist in me. I had more energy. When I felt down, bored, or uninspired, I just thought of things I was grateful for, and the negative feelings evaporated. When I had tried meditation, I had been unable to let go of negative thoughts. The gratitude list cured me of that problem. Nowadays, I follow up each day's gratitude list with ten minutes of meditation. I simply "watch" my mind. I can observe my cravings without getting caught by or sucked into them.

Some of us recovering addicts become mired in negativity. Negativity takes up most of the space between our ears. In my work with cyber addicts, I have found that breaking the attachment to negativity is best accomplished through daily gratitude practice.

Whenever I have a particularly intense craving to play a video game or find myself starting to get lost on the Internet, I pull out pen and paper and write down the things in my life for which I am grateful. Then, I write down my goals. This listing process does something to my brain. It jump-starts me out of emotional malaise and brings balance. After all the things I have tried, surprisingly, it is the simple things that have helped me most.

Scientists are now confirming my findings. In a study of organ recipients, researchers found that patients who kept gratitude journals scored higher on "measures of mental health, general health and vitality than those who kept only routine notes about their days."[1] Robert Emmons, a University of California–Davis professor who specializes in the study of gratitude, found that "increased feelings of gratitude can cause people's well-being and quality of life to improve."[2] I recommend a gratitude journal to everyone, especially those struggling to recover from addiction.

My daily meditation and gratitude practices, a few key mentors, and a burning desire to achieve my goals have kept me on the path. My example, I think, underscores the need for perseverance. If we keep at recovery, we will find what we are looking for.

Kyle's Story: Rekindling Passion

Kyle, whom we met in the first chapter, had been active in sports and played leading roles in high school and community theater before entering college. He pulled back from the theater soon after high school because he believed that he would never make it as a star, and thus saw no point in continuing. A few months later in college, a serious injury prevented him from playing sports. Stripped of the two loves of his life, he spiraled downward toward depression. A computer game took center stage in his life. He played daily for at least seven hours, skipped classes, missed work, and ignored his friends. He and his parents came to see me because he had flunked out. They wanted to develop a program for academic success.

Kyle had never dealt with the intense feelings that came from losing the two most important activities in his life. "I feel like crap most of the time," he told me, "but my game is the only thing that makes me forget about my problems." I sent him to a therapist to work out his emotional issues before trying to help him with gaming. After a few months, he started to attend one of my weekly support groups because he wanted to stop gaming. His work with the therapist had made him realize that he was addicted. But he was unsuccessful at stopping on his own.

In the group, Kyle consistently expressed sadness about the loss of his former life. "My life used to have purpose," he said. "I want that back." Every week for months, the group challenged Kyle to find a way to play sports and get involved in acting.

He finally volunteered at a children's theater project. He threw himself into the job. "I'm starting to feel energized like I used to," he told us. His dedication to the job resulted in the offer of a paid position. Now, he works part-time and is going to school to become a teacher. He wants to teach drama and perhaps coach soccer. "I've got my 'mojo' back," Kyle told the group. "Theater and sports are in my blood, and I have to do something with them."

His cravings for his game linger, but he has not given in to them. "Whenever I feel a strong urge to play the game," he said, "I think about those kids and how much they need me." This sense of purpose has propelled Kyle out of his addiction. He still attends a gaming addiction support group. "Coming to the group helps keep me sober," Kyle said. "It makes me feel good about myself too, when I help another recovering addict. It reminds me of how far I've come and makes me really commit to never going back."

Kyle came out of the escapism of his addiction and began to deal with his underlying emotional issues. Once he stopped running from his feelings, he could actually start working on them. He found extensive support and developed a program of recovery that worked for him. More important, he reignited passion in his life. He devoted himself to a pursuit that gave his life meaning and allowed him to connect with other people. He found sustenance for himself by helping others.

Kyle's example demonstrates that ending the addictive behavior is only a small part of recovery. Entering recovery is the beginning of a lifelong path.

Jake's Story: Be All You Can Be!

Like Kyle, many addicted gamers struggle to find a sense of purpose. They know they have a great deal of talent but can find no suitable way to channel it. They see themselves as Sir Lancelot before he found King Arthur, cursed by not being able to find a king worthy of their service. They want to be more involved in the world, but their efforts come up short. Some, like Kyle, suffer from emotional difficulties, while others simply never find an activity—other than gaming—that engages them. If they have a job, it is often pure drudgery, because employment seems an unfortunate distraction from the game.

Jake, a twenty-one-year-old unrepentant slacker, lived with his mother and acquired and lost jobs every few months. His irregular sleep habits made it difficult to get up in the morning, so he was often late and sometimes did not even show up for work. World of Warcraft and Command & Conquer controlled his life. He came to one of my groups off and on for a few months but did not commit to recovery.

One day, on a whim, he showed up at an Army recruiter's office. He told the sergeant his story. Much to Jake's surprise, the recruiter declared: "You're perfect for the Army. The battlefield tracking system we use is a lot like Command & Conquer, except that you don't get to control the whole battlefield."

Jake was stunned by the man's fluency in video game jargon. He learned that the recruiter had, like him, done poorly in high school and had struggled with gaming addiction. He told Jake, "The Army allowed me to turn an addiction into an asset. You're going to find that most of the guys you serve with are big-time video gamers."

That recruiter was telling the truth. I have done extensive interviews with soldiers who served in Iraq. One artillery section chief told me, "There's not much to do in Iraq. Everyone in our platoon played Madden [a football video game], and we even rigged up a Nintendo 64 emulator." Nearly all the recruiters I talk to tell me that a good many of their recruits play video games.

The United States Army has, for at least the last ten years, been aware of the value of video games for recruitment and training of soldiers. Many training modules rely on video games to teach military skills. Larry McCracken, a captain in the U.S. Navy, says that, "Video games make better soldiers and sailors faster, safer, and cheaper. The realism you get has the ability to keep somebody engaged and playing a game for three or four hours, as opposed to [learning] in a classroom, where after fifteen minutes they're bored."[3]

The U.S. Army launched its own game, America's Army, to give players a basic test drive of life in the Army. The game "provides players with the most authentic military experience available, from exploring the development of soldiers in individual and collective training to their deployment in simulated missions in the War on Terror."[4] Many gamers who have played this simulation have enlisted. On occasion, players have even applied skills learned from the America's Army game to real-life situations.

On November 23, 2007, Paxton Galvanek, a young man who had happened to play as a medic in the game America's Army, was driving in North Carolina when he witnessed a sport-utility vehicle flip about five times.[5] As his wife phoned for help, Galvanek assumed the role of first responder as he approached the smoking vehicle. Needing to get them out fast, he first helped the passenger out of the truck. The passenger had minor cuts and injuries. Galvanek told him to stay back and went quickly to the driver, who he pulled to safety on the side of the road. The Army's Web site contains a detailed account of the incident:

> Using knowledge he learned from playing America's Army, Galvanek knew he had to prioritize the situation, choosing which of the wounded travelers would need to be tended to immediately. "I remember vividly in section four of the game's medic training, during the field medic scenarios, I had to evaluate the situation and place priority on the more critically wounded," Galvanek said. "In the case of this accident, I evaluated the situation and placed priority on the driver of the car,

who had missing fingers." The driver of the vehicle had lost two fingers in the accident and was bleeding profusely. He had also suffered head trauma. Galvanek used what he learned from the game to give immediate aid to the driver.[6]

By the time the ambulance arrived, the victims were already stable. Galvanek had treated the passenger, who had minor scrapes and lacerations, and also stopped profuse bleeding from the driver who had two fingers severed. Doctors and paramedics agreed that Galvanek had used correct procedures and had prevented serious medical complications. With its video game, it seems that the Army has tapped into a powerful teaching tool that actually saves lives.

Many video gamers, like Jake, join the Army and find an organization that makes use of their unique skills. Jake said it was like entering a different world. From basic training to his present duty in Iraq, Jake has felt at home in the Army. "This is the first time in my life that I have really felt valued," Jake told me. "I thought I was destined to be a loser for the rest of my life."

Although he cannot tell me exactly what he does, the young man who had a 1.4 grade point average in high school now has top secret security clearance. He does something involving computer servers, and his superiors have been more than satisfied with his performance. He has been promoted several times. Before he enlisted, he could not hold a job. He now has a skill set that should command a generous wage when he goes back to civilian life.

Certainly, I credit the Army for Jake's success, but at a more fundamental level, Jake is successful because he has been able to channel his talent. He has found an environment in which he thrives. Jake was computer-savvy from about age seven. His aptitude for computers was, however, swallowed up by gaming.

"If I had had some computer classes when I was young," Jake told me, "maybe I wouldn't have had to go to Iraq to find success." Jake thinks it is important for parents of computer-oriented children to get their kids involved in advanced computer classes and summer programs at an early age. "Kids who are like I was need to know that they have incredible skills. The world runs on computers and desperately needs people like us."

Ken's Story: Dealing with Your Issues

Ken went into therapy for several years once he realized that there were some things amiss with how he related to others. While providing him with some answers, however, therapy did not solve his problems. "After about six months, I came to the conclusion that I had the wrong attitude with my therapist," Ken said. "I started to realize that I was going there because I liked having someone listen to me talk about my problems for an hour." Ken linked his attitude toward therapy with how he treated his friends. "One of the things that I do with my friends is that I just go on and on about myself, assuming that everyone is interested. When the other person is talking, I am already planning the next thing that I'm going to say." Therapy and MySpace allowed Ken to have a captive audience to talk about himself. But once he started taking a careful look at himself, he realized that in interactions with real people, this tendency was pushing people away. "My father used to rant at and lecture me," Ken said. "It was a sad day when I finally admitted that I was doing this to some extent to other people." Coming out of denial about this behavior was the start of the process for Ken. He continued therapy, but he also got involved in some support groups. One was a men's-issues group and the other was for Adult Children of Alcoholics (Ken's father was an alcoholic). These support groups were perfect for Ken because they forced him to listen to other people, while allowing him a forum to discuss and get advice on his own problems. He took steps to confront his problems, rather than escape from them into the cyber world. He has continued to attend different types of support groups because he finds that they help him stay on track in the important relationships in his life. He has even found some passion, having become an occasional group facilitator of one of the groups. I can attest to this because since he has been attending them, he has become a more attentive friend to me!

Tony's Story: Battling the Enemy Within

"It's hard to fight an enemy who has outposts in your head."
—Sally Kempton, author and meditation teacher

Tony was a textbook video game addict. Like many of the addicts you have already read about, he played his game, World of Warcraft (WoW), with wild abandon. The beneficiary of a trust fund, Tony had no financial worries, nor did he have anyone to nag him. He had moved away from his family and put little effort into making friends. Living a life that many gamers dream about, Tony nevertheless began to feel something was wrong.

His whole life revolved around the game, and his only social interaction was with members of his in-game guild. "They were my family," Tony said. "I played on the same server with essentially the same people for almost two years."

And then, he moved to China. Tony's uncle offered him a financial package that Tony could not refuse. He took a position overseeing his uncle's business affairs in the Far East. "I was half way around the world and that meant a serious lag on my computer if I played on the American server," Tony said. "I could not continue playing WoW unless I joined the Oceanic servers. And none of my friends were there."

Tony became depressed, largely due to the separation from his friends. He could not even chat with them online because when they were playing, he was working.

Tony was desperate to do something about the depression. "I guess I had been depressed for a long time," Tony told me, "but without WoW to occupy all my time, I finally was forced to feel it." At the urging of a concerned coworker, Tony took up jujutsu, a Japanese martial art.

He took to it right away. "Nothing beats the adrenaline rush of sparring with another person," Tony said. "Nothing is more exhilarating than mustering all my strength to throw down a person who is trying with all his might to do the same to me." For Tony, the thrill of real combat trumped that found in the cyber world.

Tony confessed, "If I didn't have jujutsu when I came back to the States, I would definitely have gone back to WoW. Now, I am finally in therapy and dealing with my depression rather than avoiding it." Tony summed it up: "In the game, I was fighting every day but was avoiding the real monster, the constant depression I have felt my whole life. Now that I am dealing with the real enemy, I don't need the game anymore."

Tony's story illustrates that for some, cyber addiction is not the primary issue, but is a symptom that masks other problems.

Meeting Makers Make It

Tony, Ken, and Jake demonstrate the importance of helping cyber addicts find some passion in their lives. I facilitate three cyber game addiction support groups a week that are designed to do just that. In my groups, we do not work the Twelve Steps per se, although some members pursue a Twelve Step model of recovery on their own. My groups are structured to move addicts into lives of purpose. The groups are designed not only to support the cessation of the addiction, but also to help members discover their passion and empower them to follow it.

The meetings are divided into four rounds.[7] Round one is the listening round. Each of us takes a turn talking about the struggles and triumphs of our week. We encourage and honor successes but offer no feedback. This round is an opportunity to check in on our goals, stretches, and challenges from the previous week. Round one is an exchange of information.

During round two, members may invite feedback. Because we are all addicts, we can often detect a lack of authenticity or if the member is trying to deceive the group or him- or herself. "When you said that just now," one member told another, "I got the sense that you weren't giving us the whole story." The member who receives the feedback is encouraged to listen and not become defensive. The group practices the art of giving and receiving feedback, which goes a long way toward improving interpersonal skills.

Round three brings stretches and goals. Each member takes a few minutes to talk about long-term goals and the specific steps he or she will take during the coming week to attain them. Sometimes members challenge each other during this round, asking for clarity and sometimes encouraging fellow members to aim higher with their goals. Participants are asked to stretch, challenging themselves to move out of their comfort zone.

In round four, we reaffirm our commitment to call someone from the group if we "get into trouble" before the next meeting. In addition, we commit to calling a specific group member at least twice over the coming week to check in. The goal is to apply what we learn in the group to our lives.

The groups have been remarkably successful. The combination of ongoing support, compassionate feedback, and empowerment to achieve goals propels addicts into a new way of living. People who keep coming to the group keep moving forward in their lives. The Twelve Step maxim, "meeting makers make it," is quite accurate.

A Word of Caution

The group approach does not work for everybody. Further, I can make no recommendation for treatment of individuals I have never met. I advise, first and foremost, that parents or loved ones of a cyber addict seek the advice of a doctor or therapist before making any decisions on treatment. As with any other addiction, treatment depends totally on individual circumstances. No one should use this book as a diagnostic manual.

Addiction, in its many forms, is a pernicious issue that requires thoughtful consideration. Reading a book on the subject is not a replacement for professional help and intervention. I discuss successful approaches, but only to provide the reader with knowledge of some of the many treatment styles used to help video gaming addiction. Do not consider this book a substitute for professional help.

Online Help for Online Addicts

"The most brilliant minds in the world can be found wasting their lives in front of computer screens," my friend Liz Woolley said. "Many of the world's problems would be quickly solved if those folks could just find a way to stay away from their games."

Liz has firsthand experience about talent wasted because of computer gaming. She lost her son, Shawn, in 2001. He committed suicide in front of the computer screen, and his unfortunate mother discovered his body. Shawn's EverQuest game was still running. Her son had struggled with a variety of issues, but Liz believes the game threw him over the edge and played a major role in his death. Although the makers of EverQuest, the Sony Corporation, have denied that the game contributed to Shawn's death,[8] Liz was determined to tell the world her side of the story.

She decided that she wanted to help others avoid the pain that gaming had brought on her family. She created On-Line Gamers Anonymous (OLGA), a network of support groups for addicted video gamers and their loved ones. The group operates on the premise that excessive gaming often becomes an addiction and may be a symptom of serious underlying mental or emotional problems. The organization does not crusade against a particular game, but seeks instead to educate the public and gamers about the dangers of excessive video gaming. Liz told me, "We just want to let addicted gamers know that they are not alone."

In the tradition of the Twelve Steps, the organization conducts regular meetings and gives its members access to support from people all over the world. The daily meetings take place online, a medium with which addicted gamers are intimately acquainted. The group's Web site features articles, message boards, references for professional intervention, and tips for recovery from video gaming addiction. The group adds ten new members every day.

I have participated in OLGA meetings as part of my recovery and have talked with many members to share our stories. Many addicted gamers have successfully made use of OLGA to stop gaming and to stay in recovery. For me, there is something uniquely healing about using the computer and the Internet for recovery as opposed to using them as vehicles for indulging an addiction. I strongly recommend that anyone touched by video gaming addiction visit the OLGA Web site, www.olganon.org. You will find understanding, support, and compassion. One word of caution is that some people at OLGA have a one-size-fits-all approach. I reiterate that cyber addictions are often just one of many problems that addicts struggle with. Many issues lurk below the surface, and it is important to seek the advice of trained professionals, such as therapists, social workers, addiction counselors, and doctors. Every cyber addict is unique, a fact which necessitates professional advice and consent when making any decisions regarding treatment.

Inpatient Treatment

Some clients have gone into inpatient treatment centers for recovery. Residential treatment options allow the time, space, and isolation for individuals to begin dealing with their emotional issues. Such intensive treatment options require extensive support after the addict returns home. Therapists and support groups are crucial. If the addict comes back to the same family situation and is once again surrounded by the same temptations without significant support, relapse is all but assured.

While treatment centers for Internet-based addictions are well established in other parts of the world, such as Japan, Taiwan, Holland, China, and South Korea, in the United States such treatment is still in the infancy stages. Only a handful of inpatient facilities currently specialize in cyber addiction, and most medical insurance carriers do not cover extensive stays. Also, most therapists who deal with other addictions are not tech-savvy enough to understand the problem, and studies regarding the effectiveness of treatment centers largely rely on centers self-reporting.[9] The world is waking up to the enormity of the problem, but much work is left to be done. (See "Resources" for a sampling of current U.S. inpatient facilities.)

In emergency situations, community mental health facilities are an option, but patients are usually released after a twenty-four- to seventy-two-hour emergency psychiatric hold.

Total Separation or Controlled Use?

Some people are able to use technology to support their recovery, while some cyber addicts require total separation from the electronic universe.

It is significantly easier for alcoholics to avoid bars and liquor stores, or for gambling addicts to avoid casinos, than it is for cyber junkies to avoid the ubiquity of computers and video game systems. The vast majority of jobs, for example, require computer use to some extent, putting cyber addicts in daily temptation with their addictive behavior of choice. I, for example, must use email to keep in touch with clients and other professionals. This is unavoidable. Young people who struggle to get their cyber behaviors under control have to use computers to complete homework or perform research for school projects, and when they spend time with their friends, the latest video game or social developments displayed on Facebook are likely topics of conversation.

Cyber addictions are more akin to food addictions in that both types involve an inescapable facet of life with which we must contend. In the early days of my recovery, I avoided all video games and used to time myself on the computer, allowing just enough time to check email. After the first six months, I began to refine my approach. I experimented and realized that I did not have a problem with most video games. I can play all types of games except real-time strategy games, and I have no interest in online multiplayer fantasy games such as World of Warcraft. So, when I am running a study group for individuals with ADHD, we often take game breaks and play Nintendo 64 games together. I feel no addictive pull. I can play for fifteen minutes and be perfectly content. Each individual, with honesty and integrity, must decide what recovery means for him or her. Ideally, this determination will be made with the wise counsel of trusted friends and family.

As far as social networking and online chatting are concerned, I put myself on a timer (no more than thirty minutes per day). Facebook is incredibly useful for networking with potential clients and other professionals and has helped to get the word out about my book. It has also connected me with many people from my past. Online chatting allows me to keep in touch with three friends around the world free of charge, but I strictly limit chatting beyond them, not permitting myself to add new friends unless there is a compelling need. One such case involved a researcher in Hungary who was doing a study on video gaming addiction. She and I kept in touch and shared information through Yahoo! Messenger.

I have been in recovery for many years and have developed a strong internal sense of when I am on the verge of going into the addictive zone. In my opinion, I have become quite adept at discerning this, but early in recovery, it is important for addicts to have supportive friends and family members with whom we can talk about the potential for certain situations to lead to relapse. If we have to use a computer, it is useful to have a timer so that we can become more conscious about how much time is spent. Commitment to stay off certain sites or away from certain games must be adhered to, and it can be very helpful to have a person to take a weekly inventory with. It is crucial to examine our behavior and the support that we use on a weekly basis as a way of assessing the success of the recovery program and making any needed adjustments. Relapse is best prevented when addicts have a robust network of support.

Relapse

Even with successful treatment, relapse is a fact of life when dealing with addiction. I relapsed many times during my early attempts to stop gaming. Then, when I had finally found a way to avoid playing video games excessively, addiction reared its head in my life again—I relapsed into online chatting. Although this was a different behavior and so may not be considered a true relapse by some purists, the addictive component was remarkably similar to that underlying my video gaming compulsion.

I think I will always be more susceptible to addictions, which is why part of my recovery is constant vigilance. I expect that any day could be the one that leads me down that dark path yet again. In spite of impulses to stop my gratitude lists, meditation, and emotional healing work, I know that these practices significantly decrease the likelihood of slipping back.

Addiction gets hardwired into the brain, as discussed earlier, and for that reason can function as somewhat of a default, constantly tempting the addictively prone person to fall. It is crucial that we addicts do not become overconfident in our recovery and recognize that relapse is a very real danger. If we expect it, we can prevent it. Through my own journey and in my work with others, I have found some signs that should raise red flags.

1. **Showing less interest in friends and family.** Keeping our support system of friends and family close is imperative. Without them, we surely are at risk. Whenever we begin to isolate, the alarm should sound. It is time to get some more support and find a way to draw friends and family closer.

2. **Being overconfident.** Just like me during my first attempt at stopping my video game habit, many addicts come to a place where they think they can do it alone. This is a very dangerous mindset and often leads to relapse.

3. **Major life changes.** Divorce, graduation, unemployment, job-switching, breakup, and a variety of other factors put

us at risk for falling back into addiction. Our inability to cope with our problems in healthy ways was a major contributor to starting us down the addictive path in the first place, and these negative life events have the potential to take us back. When dealing with any major shift or change in life, it is important for addicts and their loved ones to be on the lookout for signs of relapse.

4. **Feeling bored with life.** Frequent boredom often precedes relapse into addiction. Addicts often find the routines and mundane repetition of life particularly hard to bear. Finding ways to make one's life more stimulating and exciting in healthy ways is crucial to any recovery. Lack of success in this area, however, increases the risk for relapse.

5. **Avoidance.** Lack of conflict resolution at work, at home, and in relationships is a harbinger of relapse. Given that almost all addicts use their addiction to avoid dealing with emotional issues and conflicts, not breaking this tendency puts recovery on a shaky foundation.

It is important that every recovering addict do his or her own internal growth work to break the cycle of avoidance. Surrounding oneself with loving and supportive people is also tremendously important. Stimulating and worthwhile pursuits must be found to take the place of the massive amount of time that used to be spent in cyber bliss.

If an addict does relapse, the first order of business is to tell someone. An addict must reach out and establish an interpersonal bridge. Of course, the first impulse is to cover it up and hide it. Addicts feel immense shame when they relapse, a feeling that intensifies when other people discover what they have done. But ultimately, trustworthy friends and family help us addicts heal that shame by loving us and supporting us back on the path. If we reach out, over half the battle is won. Addiction ruptures the interpersonal bridge, but being vulnerable and honest with others can quickly repair it.

My Journey Continues

Since I entered recovery, I have been able to achieve a number of my life goals. I have been in several rock bands, performed stand-up comedy, and written this book. I would have accomplished none of these if I were still lost in cyberland. Sure, I relapsed several times, but on each of these occasions, I reached out to trusted friends who helped me get back up.

Many traditional Twelve Step recovery programs advocate helping the "addict who still suffers." I'm not working a Twelve Step program, but I am nonetheless committed to helping other cyber addicts into recovery because, among many reasons, I believe that we are an uncommonly creative group. It troubles me to think of how much of our talent goes to waste as we sit idle in front of computer or TV screens. When we succeed in channeling our creative energies, we do great deeds. I have been heartened to see recovering cyber addicts fight for our country overseas, serve in the Peace Corps, tutor inner-city children, and become successful in any number of careers. We recovering cyber addicts are a capable group when we find inspiration.

CHAPTER 7

a guide for loved ones

"To bring up a child in the way he should go,
travel that way yourself once in a while."

Josh Billings, nineteenth-century humorist

Many parents and spouses see video gaming as a black hole that sucks in their loved ones and maintains an unbreakable hold. One mother told me, "I just don't understand how he can sit in front of a computer screen for eight hours." She struggled to make sense of what seemed to her an unthinkable squandering of potential. "Where would the world be if Edison and Einstein had sat in front of a computer screen all day?" she bellowed with increasing frustration, incensed at her son's ability to tune her out.

This mother was at a loss as to how to solve this problem. Often, she simply did nothing, because none of her efforts have had any lasting effect. When she hid the computer, he found a way to play at school, the library, and at a friend's house. She offered monetary bribes, but her sixteen-year-old son did not seem to need any money. She begged and pleaded, took him to a psychiatrist, and threatened to send him to an inpatient mental health facility. When she followed through on that threat, the doctors wouldn't take him because he performed brilliantly at the intake interview. He convinced the doctors that his mother was the one with the problem. She now feels she is a failure as a parent and worries incessantly about her son's future, certain that low-paying jobs or unemployment awaits him.

"The son that I know ceases to exist when he's on that damn game," she told me, struggling not to cry. "I feel like he's been temporarily kidnapped by the characters in that hideous game," she yelled. "He's an alien to me. I do not understand him!"

If someone in your life is excessively plugged into the cyber world, you undoubtedly want to help. Yet starting down this path invariably brings up a great deal of fear and anxiety. This endeavor is a grueling process that requires extensive support. As you take the steps toward helping your child or adult loved one with a cyber addiction, be cautious and plan thoroughly. Remember: you are dealing with a condition that is likely hard-wired into the brain of the addict. Addictions are persistent and incredibly hard to give up, and addicts are prone to relapse. This chapter will walk you through some ways to help your loved one as well as discuss what to avoid in your efforts to help.

Is There an Addict in the House?

During my years of active cyber addiction, I had isolated myself and cloaked my behaviors to such an extent that no one besides two close friends had a clue about my problems. I benefited from these men with whom I was neither living nor intimately involved. Although I got angry with them at certain times, usually I did not feel threatened.

When dealing with an addict in your own home, however, the dynamics are much more complex. If you have to live with the addict, child or adult, confrontation certainly has its place. We must communicate to the addict that we take exception to his or her behaviors. We must tell the addict of the risks that he or she is running. At some point, it may become necessary to draw a line and spell out the consequences of continued addictive behavior. When that line is crossed, follow-through becomes crucial.

HELPING OR ENABLING?

Through well-intentioned efforts, perhaps even out of love, family members often enable the cyber addict. They create comforts and offer amenities that keep the addict from hitting bottom. They give second chances upon second chances. The only hope for recovery is that the addict feels the full, natural consequences of the addiction, starts to realize how out of control life has become, and thus wants to change. The longer we continue to aid the addiction, the longer it will take for the addict to hit bottom.

If you recognize that some of your behaviors might be enabling, it's important to take some time for your own internal work before you make further attempts to help the addict. You have to figure out why you enable and what you need to change in yourself to be able to actually help the addict. You can begin by taking an inventory of how you may have directly or indirectly contributed to your loved one's addiction.

JOANNE'S STORY: MORE HARM THAN GOOD

Michael's grandmother informed him for about the twenty-third time, "I heard that those boys at the grocery store make good money." Michael's relatives took turns telling him about job opportunities and scolding him for not being more proactive in finding work. "He won't go to anything like that," his mother, Joanne, chimed in. "You know how many times I've tried to take him up there?" Joanne often felt under attack by her relatives for her seemingly lax parenting style. She rushed to defend Michael from their relentless disapproval, but she was also defending herself.

Joanne was a single parent in many respects, because her husband, who owned a successful business, worked twelve- to fourteen-hour days. On top of that, from the time Michael was five, his father had been finding fault with everything the boy did. Most of the interaction between father and son was negative. Joanne reacted by trying to shield the boy from his father. She would interrupt the scolding sessions by yelling at her husband and then spiriting the boy away to a distant corner of the house. She would try to soothe Michael, thinking she was undoing the damage that her husband had done.

Taking his cue from his mother, Michael avoided his father. As he moved into adolescence, he spent inordinate amounts of time in his own room. Soon, avoidance of his father turned into shirking of all responsibility. He played RuneScape for at least five hours every day and had an obsessive relationship with his Facebook profile. He did not do his household chores. His grades, which had for most of his school years been quite high, plummeted.

Predictably, Michael's father threatened consequences. He tried to confiscate Michael's Xbox and planned on taking away both of his computers. Michael's mother refused to cooperate. Bitter arguments between the parents went on for months. The inability of Michael's parents to cooperate ensured the status quo.

Finally, the family met with me for an assessment. The parents hoped I could help Michael with school and his excessive cyber usage. The first session essentially involved the parents arguing for the whole hour, each determined to place the blame on the other. I told them that before we could even think of tackling the school and cyber issues, they needed counseling to confront the dynamics operating in their family. "Michael's behavior is a symptom of the problem," I told them, "but not the root cause." Before the parents could help Michael, they needed to help themselves.

CHALLENGING THE ADDICTION

Once parents or spouses understand their involvement, they may be ready to stop supporting the addiction and begin to challenge it. Michael's parents underwent marriage counseling for a year while Michael saw his own therapist. All three went to family therapy as well. The parents committed to working on their issues, and Michael began working on his. Eventually, they developed a behavior modification plan to reward Michael for good grades. Computer and game time, access to a car, and spending money were linked to his performance in school. The plan ultimately worked because of the family's commitment to understanding the complete picture.

Not all families need such extensive therapeutic intervention. Some may simply need to assess how they enable addiction. Electricity, computers, video games, access to transportation, and a house all require money, and should all be treated as privileges that need to be earned. Familial relationships need quality time and consistent participation to flourish. If you have a teenage video game addict who can't find a job but plays games for many hours each day, then it's time to take away the computer. If you have an adult child living with you who exhibits addictive behavior, then it is time to ask him or her to leave home. If your husband spends more time on his game than with you and your children, then it is time for counseling. You must disentangle the fabric of your life from the addictive web so that you no longer allow the addict to avoid facing consequences.

REMOVING THE PROBLEM

I know of many teenagers who thwart parental attempts to rid the house of electronics. Some turn to friends for their cyber fix, while others manage to smuggle games and mini computers home and conceal them. For a determined addict, the ubiquity of video games and computers makes it easy to find a fix.

I have worked with a few teenagers who ran away from home to go to a video game house, the gaming addiction equivalent of a drug den. In one such case, Mitch, a seventeen-year-old young man addicted to World of Warcraft and Command & Conquer, moved to an inner-city neighborhood not far from home. His parents finally tracked him down to a three-bedroom apartment in a crime-ridden neighborhood that housed fourteen video game addicts, most of them unemployed. Many of them were habitual marijuana users, a feature of video gaming addiction that is becoming increasingly common.

Mitch's parents took him back home but did not know how to proceed. Mitch had no grip on reality and only primitive social skills. He hardly talked at all.

Some cyber addicts can become violent when their ability to

game is threatened. Such was the case with Josh, a sixteen-year-old who attacked and beat his father as he was removing the boy's computer from the house. There had never been a hint of violence in Josh; he had never even talked back to his parents. But to Josh, having his computer confiscated was like having a part of himself ripped out. "It was like I was being attacked," Josh told me. "I felt like I needed to protect myself. I didn't think. I just lashed out." Both Mitch and Josh needed complete separation from electronics and their families in order to shake their addictions. They were too far gone for therapy, coaching, or support groups to have any appreciable impact. They needed the cyber equivalent of detox.

For addicts like Mitch and Josh, intense intervention is needed. I have had several students and clients who turned their lives around at Outward Bound programs, which take place in wilderness settings, free from electronic intrusions. Outward Bound seeks to build character and encourage self-discovery "through challenge and adventure, and to impel [the patients] to achieve more than they ever thought possible, to show compassion for others and to actively engage in creating a better world."[1]

The organization's programs teach problem-solving, goal setting, and interpersonal communication—all skills that many cyber addicts lack. Total isolation from electronics gives participants space to reflect on their lives. The program also encourages them to find a way to contribute to their communities and make a difference in the world. (See "Resources" for contact information.)

Those who attend Outward Bound usually do so voluntarily. For those who refuse such options, therapeutic wilderness training programs may be appropriate. Aspen Education Group (AEG) has extensive experience dealing with video-game-addicted teens. In recent years, AEG has been experiencing a huge influx of young people who are checking out of life, refusing to go to school, and engaging in obsessive cyber activities.

AEG's wilderness program participants live off the land for several weeks. They become part of a small group, or "family unit," and each member is expected to carry out his or her share of family responsibilities. Privileges depend on successful completion of requirements. Interaction within the small groups develops social skills and emotional literacy. Daily group and frequent individual therapy help participants deal with their psychological issues. At the same time, the family members of a child in the program are encouraged to work on their own issues so that they can provide a healthier environment when their child returns. I have had several clients attend Aspen programs, and the success rate has been high. The cost, however, is somewhat prohibitive, but loans are available.

There are many similar wilderness programs that can be found easily on the Internet. I list Aspen because of my positive experiences with them. If you choose to explore these programs, make sure to choose one experienced specifically with cyber addictions.

In other extreme cases, I advise parents to consider a brief inpatient stay at a local community mental health facility. These places generally will only hold folks for a few days of psychiatric evaluation. This step, however, can go a long way in parents demonstrating their seriousness in confronting their child's addiction. Sometimes this tactic is enough to put the child on the right track. I have seen several teenagers change their attitudes largely as a function of wanting to avoid a psychiatric stay-over.

Before deciding on which type of treatment option is best for your loved one, talk to people outside of the program or facility you're considering. Talk to families who have had a loved one in the program and to therapists and educational consultants.

It is preferable, of course, to confront the cyber addict long before intensive treatment becomes necessary. It is important to become aware of the warning signs so that early and swift intervention is possible.

Caution

When trying to help an addict, it's important to exercise great caution. You'll accomplish much more by setting and enforcing boundaries than by yelling and criticizing. Confrontation can destroy the interpersonal bridge and push an addict's behavior more deeply underground. An addict almost always feels shameful at his or her behavior, as if he or she is flawed at a fundamental level. If your reaction as a helper triggers shame in the addict, your relationship with him or her will be damaged.

Do not underestimate the power of shame in addiction. Although we rarely admit it, we cyber addicts feel horrible about our compulsive behavior. These feelings lurk deep within us and rise to awareness once we actually admit there is a problem. Deep down, we long to stop. We possess keen minds and imaginations. We want to exercise our creative muscles. We wish we could control ourselves.

Helping an Adult Loved One

Helping an addicted loved one who is an adult can be a tricky situation, different in many ways than a parent helping a child. Of course, the spouse of a cyber addict may actually feel somewhat like a parent, prone perhaps to constant, albeit fruitless, nagging. If you realize that your adult child or your spouse is a cyber addict, the first step is to get some support. Surround yourself with a few trusted friends from whom you can solicit feedback and advice. When you're in the middle of an addictive situation, your perceptions can be skewed, especially if you have even the slightest bit of enabler in you. It is important not to rely on only one person for support and advice; with multiple people to rely on, you will attain a more balanced view of the situation, as well as ensure that you do not burn out one individual. It can also be helpful to join an addiction support group. Although I do not know of any in-person support groups for spouses/loved ones of cyber addicts, Al-Anon can be quite beneficial. Obviously, this group was started to serve the loved ones of alcoholics, but it can be very helpful for anyone who is coping with a loved one with an addiction of any kind.

The starting point for you to help your addicted loved one is to make sure that you are in no way enabling the addict. When dealing with an adult addict, taking away the computer or gaming console will not be an option in most cases. Instead, try asking yourself some questions about what's really going on: Is your loved one fulfilling family and professional obligations? Have you noticed some of the warning signs that addiction is taking hold? Is your cyber addict's behavior bringing disharmony into your life? If you answer yes to any of these questions, you need to give serious consideration to taking some action. In addition to your support network, which should be firmly in place before any action is taken, it might behoove you to examine your own issues by making an appointment with a therapist. Such a move will help you get clear within yourself and make your subsequent decisions more firmly grounded.

With a therapist and a support network in place, you might decide that an ultimatum is the right way to go. I wouldn't try this approach on your own. It would be most beneficial to find someone with experience in organizing such an event. The best option would be to find someone with experience in interventions. This person will underscore the need to have treatment options in place before confronting the addicted individual. These could include therapy, support groups, or even a short inpatient stay in extreme cases. This book is not a guide on how to do interventions, but I do wish to reiterate exercising this option only with proper support from individuals experienced in such matters. Do not simply take matters into your own hands!

Parenting in the Age of Technology

In my practice as an ADHD and academic coach, I see many young people who spend little time on homework and studying, but enormous amounts of time on video games and the Internet. Among the kids who make their way to me, excessive video gaming and/or computer usage accompanies poor academic performance about 80 percent of the time. Friends and colleagues nationwide who do similar work have made similar findings.

Jared, a fourteen-year-old who sees me for help in school, could not manage to write down assignments in his planner. The seemingly absent-minded teen went to elaborate lengths, however, to sneak his iPhone into class and send texts to his friends. An iPhone is a touch-screen cell phone with the power of a computer. Jared was so adept with the device that he never even looked at the screen. He also concealed his phone on his lap and played video games during the school day.

His parents only discovered Jared's daytime distraction when they examined his text-messaging bills. The young man admitted his transgressions, the iPhone was taken away, and presto, his grades went up. I strongly advise against iPhones and other smartphones for teens and encourage parents to take a serious look at how much access to electronics their children have. The temptations of technology are hard to resist.

Most teens enjoy a seamless flow of technology, from the moment their cell phone alarm wakes them, to the video games they play on their iPods or cell phones on the way to school and after school, to the text messages they send to their friends as they lie in bed late at night. Many teens regularly stay up until three in the morning using instant messenger services (such as AOL Instant Messenger and Yahoo! Messenger) to chat with their friends online. They play video games on their computers as they wait for their friends to send the next instant message. Teens stay "plugged in" almost twenty-four hours a day.

In our world of electronic abundance, kids feel deprived and out-of-touch if they do not have their own computer, Xbox, cell phone, and iPod. I believe that electronic privileges should be earned through performance in school and completion of household responsibilities. Denying access to electronics may be the most powerful behavior modification tool parents have. Parents whose children neglect school and home responsibilities must harness the motivating potential of limiting their child's access to electronics.

When dealing with excessive video gaming and Internet use, parents must take into account all possible sources. These now include cell phones, computers, iPods, and access to these and other devices that kids may have through their friends. Kids are remarkably resourceful at getting access to electronics.

TALK ABOUT THE POTENTIAL PROBLEM

Early discussions about excessive video gaming and Internet use can go a long way toward preventing full-blown addiction. As with drugs and sex, it is important that parents speak frankly with their children about the potential destructive consequences. Likewise, cell phones, smartphones, and text messages should be discussed. With the nature of modern society, parents have to balance the convenience of equipping their child with cell phones with the possible consequences. Most middle school children I deal with now have cell phones, which make contact and pick-up times much more manageable. When parents first get a phone for a child, it is important to put some restrictions on it, such as no phone use during the school day, other than for emergencies, or the phone gets taken away if there are any missing assignments. Remember, most cell phone service providers offer the ability to go online and shut off phones and/or limit their use. These options must be researched and implemented. Technology is probably the greatest motivational "carrot" that parents have. It is an opportunity not to be squandered.

How is a parent to go about talking about the potential problems that the cyber world presents? As a start, parents can simply share some of the stories that they read in this book, or stories that they have heard from friends or other family members. The most important thing is that kids need to be made aware. Parents have the power to put the right messages into a child's head at an early age. I strongly encourage them to use that power.

That said, I do not advise that, as a first step, you sit your child down and have a serious meeting about the dangers of the cyber world. Kids often tune out that kind of meeting. Rather, casually talk to your child when you're driving in the car. Tell him or her a cyber story you heard that shocked you. Ask if he or she knows of anybody who has a problem similar to the one you brought up. Make the cyber world a regular topic of conversation. You might even try to follow the game industry and online technology a bit so that you can have positive conversations with your child. This will give you much greater credibility if you must have a negative conversation about your child's excessive play/use.

A body of research exists, for example, on the benefits of video game playing. Familiarize yourself with these reports, and tell your child that you're proud of the video gaming abilities and skills he or she is developing. A few of the benefits that recent studies have found include greater visual attention and spatial acuity, better hand-eye coordination, and superior grasp of technology. Be sure to balance discussions with both pros and cons. When parents focus solely on drawbacks and negatives, children usually dismiss much of what the parents say. They have finely tuned radar designed to detect an oncoming lecture.

I am well aware of this radar when I talk to kids who come to see me. I usually start seeing young people diagnosed with ADHD when they are eleven or twelve because ADHD often becomes troublesome during the middle school years. My experience and educational background has shown me that once youth with ADHD hit the teen years, they are at significantly increased risk for addiction. I share studies with my students that tell of the dangers they face from the cyber world. I show them articles and highlight the information I know they will understand. I tell them stories of those I know who turned to drugs and the havoc that it wreaked. Now, I do the same with cyber addictions, and I talk about my own struggles. In this way, I open a channel for communication.

I now have clients coming to me with stories, many of which have actually helped me write this book. They tell me about their friends' excessive video game playing, texting, and online social networking, and in the process of this exchange, they become more conscious about the possibility of addiction, and thus less likely to get hooked.

Talk to your kids! I have put together some methods, described below, which have proven valuable in my years dealing with this issue. Be warned that you may need to change your parenting style. Setting limits is never fun, but if you do not set limits, your children will likely have trouble setting their own.

I have included successes and failures so that you might develop a sense of what works and the methods your child might employ to circumvent your new rules. Many parents use some of the strategies listed here in combination.

IF YOU CAN'T BEAT THEM, JOIN THEM

My familiarity with the cyber world allows me, a forty-one-year-old man, to connect with teenagers in ways that would otherwise be impossible. The cyber world makes up a serious portion of recreational time for today's youngsters. If we adults do not educate ourselves about this aspect of our culture, we will be clueless about a significant aspect of youth culture.

When youngsters first come to my ADHD study groups, they are astonished that after they complete a certain amount of work, I will play Nintendo 64 games with them. I particularly like Mario Kart, NFL Blitz 2000, and Super Smash Bros. Four players can play any of these games at one time, and we make it a social event. Sometimes we even have tournaments. I am at their level, taking the games as seriously as they do. Perhaps I'll even playfully talk trash to other players or protest to the television screen when I swear that I pressed the right button, but my guy didn't move, which resulted in my premature "death."

I also play games that I do not particularly like and that I do not play well. This gaming allows *them* to teach and mentor *me*. Again, this brings me to their level and increases my credibility as someone they can talk to.

I also use Facebook and texting to keep in touch with kids who come to see me for ADHD. I use the types of communication that they prefer, making my messages more effectively received. Some of my students even have a Facebook group called The Kevin Roberts Fan Club.

Parents need to foster a situation in which their children will listen. Youngsters are repeatedly lectured to and schooled in what is appropriate and what is not. They are experts at tuning out adults. To change that, getting to their level once in a while is crucial. Entering their video game world presents us with an excellent opportunity.

Get a Facebook account and at least familiarize yourself with the system. Your child may not want to be friends with you on Facebook, but you can still be up on the latest developments.

Find some games that you like, or just sit down and watch your child play. Ask questions like: What does this button do? Why does my guy keep falling off the cliff? Why did you go down that tunnel? How do you stop yourself from going out of control around those curves?

As a friend of mine found out with his son, be careful not to ask too many questions, however, because your child may get annoyed. You have to cultivate a genuine interest, because children can smell a lack of authenticity, which pushes them away.

I know of no more effective way to bridge the generation gap than through video games. Unfortunately, simply connecting and communicating with your excessive gamer may not be enough to get him or her to limit play time.

RESTRICT SCREEN TIME

When game time or computer usage becomes excessive—more than an hour or two per day—restrictions must be considered. Obviously, this suggestion is easier made than done. To restrict screen time, you will need to commit to tough love because if potential for wiggle room exists, kids will find it. Chances are that if you are reading this book in order to learn how to help your child reduce screen time, you have already tried—unsuccessfully—to curtail it. If you have trouble setting limits or being the "bad guy," you must deal with those issues before you attempt to create change in your children. One of my favorite Twelve Step maxims says: "Do your own work before you try to help someone else." You have to go into this process with strength and resolve.

One of the best ways to limit screen time is to have children earn it. Be aware that in embarking on this endeavor, you are bucking a social trend. Sociologists sometimes refer to today's kids as the entitlement generation. Youngsters often view electronics as a God-given right. Be prepared for strong resistance.

There are some special considerations in this area. For instance, you may want your child to carry a cell phone for communication with you. If you give your child an iPhone, then obviously this device would give access to games and the Internet. It would be wise, therefore, to purchase a low-tech phone. In addition, most cell phone companies allow you to restrict usage and even turn off the phone via the Internet. Before you purchase a phone for your child, check with your service provider and see which options are available.

When it comes to the computer, video games, and television, some parents, in great frustration, eliminate all these devices from the home. Sometimes, such drastic measures are necessary. Of course, in such cases, parents themselves are willingly limiting their own access to electronics in the interest of helping their child.

Whatever steps are ultimately taken, it is important to sit down and logically think through a system and try to conceive of how your child may try to get around it. Kids are remarkably crafty.

SCREEN TIME AS A REWARD: A DETAILED PLAN

Youngsters feel entitled to electronics. It is something to do when they can find nothing more interesting. Once video game systems and computers are brought into the home, they are usually at your child's disposal whenever he or she chooses. This easy availability has to change. Electronic amusements must be turned into a privilege to be earned, because a cyber junkie invariably neglects responsibilities at home and school. Obviously, this approach has the potential to teach valuable life lessons. You have to ask yourself what types of behaviors you want to encourage in your child. If performance in school is the issue, link video game time with good grades. If you think your child needs to be more responsible around the house, then the linkage could be with completion of chores.

For one boy whose family came to see me, screen time was linked to treating his mother with respect. If he respected his mother on one day (not yelling at her or making snide remarks), he would receive an hour and a half of screen time the following day. Interestingly, when this plan worked and fighting over excessive cybering was eliminated as an issue, the relationship between mother and son improved remarkably.

There are many different approaches to reduce a child's excessive screen time. Here are the steps that I think work best:

Step 1: Communicate that there's a problem
Tell your child that you have concerns about the amount of time he or she is spending playing video games or at the computer. Say that you are worried and that you may take away the game/ computer or phone if he or she fails to make some changes. Leave it at that and wait a while, perhaps a few weeks. This approach prevents your child from feeling blindsided and allows the idea that he or she may lose his or her cyber privileges to sink in. If the child knows restriction is coming, implementing the plan will proceed more smoothly. Do not nag. Action, not admonishment, is what the situation calls for. Say nothing more until Step 2.

Step 2: Remove game system or computer
After some time has elapsed, if your child has not significantly changed, take the video game system or computer and hide it. A

bedroom closet may suffice, but if you have a sneaky child, you may want to put it in the trunk of your car. When the child comes home from school, he or she will be very upset and may demand the return of the video game system or computer. This time will be difficult, but remain calm. When the child finds that the game system or computer is missing, he or she may call you at work. Simply tell him or her that you will have a meeting about how to get the game system back and end the discussion.

Step 3: *The system*
You need to come up with a system that links desired outcomes with the privilege of playing video games. You can use a spreadsheet, a poster, or simply a piece of paper with desired behaviors on one side and rewards on the other. It is useful to make copies so you can have a new sheet at the beginning of each week. The first step is to figure out which positive behaviors and outcomes you want to encourage in your child. Here are some examples: Achieves higher grades on tests; Completes and turns in assignments on time; Cleans his or her room without being asked; Does his or her chores without being asked; Gets three As on his or her report card; Shows respectful behavior toward parents; Plays an educational (math, reading, etc.) computer game.

Make your list pretty detailed and offer your child a variety of opportunities to earn screen time, but set a firm daily limit that cannot generally be surpassed. Perhaps allow him or her to earn up to one to two hours during the week and maybe up to four hours on Saturday or Sunday. Let your child bank time, but only let him or her withdraw a specified maximum amount of that time per day. If, for example, at the end of one week, your child did not use all the time he or she had earned, that amount of time would carry over to the next week.

Once you have figured out the behaviors you want to encourage and the accompanying rewards, write up the agreement. I recommend making it look official.

Three As on report card	Unlimited screen game time for two weekends.*
A on a math test	2 hours
Homework done without asking (must be verified)	30 minutes
Thirty-minute bike ride	30 minutes
No missed assignments for the whole week	3 hours
Cleaning bedroom without being asked	45 minutes
Doing chores without being asked	30 minutes
Respectful behavior to Mom	45 minutes

*This reward obviously is an exception to the daily time limit.
Maximum screen time per day: one hour during the week and four hours on the weekend.

This chart is simply an example; I encourage you to come up with a system that works for your individual situation.

Step 4: The meeting

At the meeting, show your child the plan for earning screen time. Communicate your firm resolve that things are going to change. Be creative and be flexible. It may take a few drafts before you realize what works to motivate your child. Also, allow your child input so that he or she feels ownership in the system. Your child may say that some rewards aren't good enough. If the suggestion seems reasonable, go along with it. Be sure to let your child know that you will be watching how well the plan works and you may set up another meeting to discuss changes.

Step 5: Agree on the plan and post it

When the final draft of the plan is polished, parents and child sign it and it goes on the refrigerator (or other highly visible common area). Also, you must make up a tracking sheet on which you keep track of rewards earned and screen time used.

You may want to allow for exceptions to the daily limit for special events, such as your child having a friend sleep over. Of course, your child would have to have earned enough screen time credit to allow for extended use. After the signed agreement and tracking chart go up on the refrigerator or wall, ceremoniously bring back the computer or video game system, but allow no playing until credit is earned.

Step 6: Monitor your child's screen time

If you think you can trust your child, leave the computer system or game console where it normally is located. If you think your child will break the rules when no one is watching, here are a few remedies that work:

- Take the computer cord or game console power cord. Your child will have to come to you to get it. This will make monitoring easier. If you have a sneaky child, he or she may find the power cord if you leave it in the house. Keep it in your car's trunk.

- Some children have managed to get their own power cords and hide them in their rooms. To beat this trick, go to this Web site: www.tvallowance.com and purchase the Television Time Manager. This device allows the TV or game console to be plugged into a lock box. The lock box then plugs into the outlet. You program the maximum amount of time that your child is allowed on the TV, computer, or game system (the device allows each of your children to have his or her own code). The cover resists tampering and the backup battery prevents resetting by unplugging and then plugging back in. The first unit you buy costs $99, and additional units are $79. I have recommended this device to many parents. It works well.

- If you need a more affordable option, put the whole game system in your trunk or in a locked room.

Step 7: Positive reinforcement
If your program works out and your child exhibits positive behavioral changes, make sure you reinforce them by noticing. Addictive behaviors become ingrained because of their involvement
in our brain's built-in reward system. Children must be reminded
often of their successes so that positive behavior becomes more
firmly rooted. Parents often fall into the trap of only noticing
the negative. Be vigilant, and for every negative you notice, find
five positives.

Step 8: Do not neglect Step 7

Step 9: Positive activities
Encourage your child to explore interests other than ones involving a video game or computer: biking, arts and crafts, martial
arts, sports, spending time with friends. You need to help your
child replace the time that he or she spent in front of a screen
with other, more beneficial activities. I recommend physical activity because cyber activities are sedentary.

There are now some aerobic video games available, which
incorporate dance and movement into the game play. You may
want to think about making exceptions to the daily screen time
limit if your child chooses one of these options. You have to work
to encourage your child into greater social interaction and physical exertion. Giving screen time credit for noncomputer activities
such as biking or sports is encouraged.

One twelve-year-old young man, Tyler, was hooked on squad
level shooting games like Call of Duty. Tyler's father got him interested in paintball, which became a biweekly father-and-son
activity. Tyler did not stop playing video games but, after a few
months of paintball, his father noticed that the boy tired more
quickly of video games, and it became easier to get him off a game.

The father of Will, a discovery-oriented eleven-year-old
addicted gamer, started taking his son on adventure bike rides.
They joined a group of urban explorers who regularly rode
through rarely seen parts of the city of Detroit, like old industrial

sections, unused railroad networks, and historic districts. Will loved it. His father bought a GPS which they used to plan rides all through the metro area. Will's father found a way to engage the boy's love of discovery in real time. He also got him out of the house for some much-needed exercise.

Your efforts to curtail your child's video game time will only be as successful as your efforts to engage your child's passions with real-time activities.

ANDY'S STORY: ANYTHING FOR A FIX

"Get off that goddamned game," I heard Andy's mother shriek. I put the phone down for a second to allow my ear to recover. Barb, a divorced mother, came to me for help with her son's school work. We became close friends as a result of our extraordinary efforts to get that kid off games.

Andy had been diagnosed with leukemia when he was eight, and doctors had not given Barb much hope, other than a highly toxic and experimental combination of chemotherapy drugs. Andy was not expected to keep up with his homework because they didn't think he was going to live. He was given a video game system, which quickly became his best friend.

A social worker recommended that, in certain games, Andy think of the bad guys as the cancerous cells in his blood. Killing the bad guys, the worker reasoned, would give Andy a sense of power over the disease. Andy pursued this suggestion with enthusiasm. Even when you talk to him today, he credits video games with the success of his treatment. "Video games gave me hope," he says. "They made me feel that I could beat the disease." It took two years of treatment, loss of hair, almost continuous nausea, and several bouts of anemia for Andy to beat the disease. He has not had a recurrence in more than twelve years.

The therapeutic benefit of video games ended when Andy's treatment came to a close. Unfortunately, his passion for games persisted. First it was Nintendo 64. His mother curtailed his use of that system when she simply took it away from him. He was only eleven at the time, and it was easy to control him. Then it was Ultima Online, an early multiplayer fantasy game that Andy started playing when he was thirteen. Barb saw disturbing signs from then on.

Andy would ask to go to the library to study, an odd request for a homework-averse thirteen-year-old. After a few weeks, his mother stopped in and talked to the librarian: "We catch him playing some dungeons and dragons game all the time," she told Barb. Andy would be invited to sleep over at friends' houses, but he would quickly make his way to their computers and ignore the friend. He never figured out why he was rarely invited back.

In high school, the problem grew worse as Andy's cunning in circumventing his mother's "no video games in my house" rule improved. This young man with a superior IQ showed early academic promise, but by the age of seventeen he had flunked out. He blamed his teachers and the school's "simplistic" curriculum. At that point, he was out of control. His mother could not prevent the strapping young man from doing as he pleased, and he was prone to fits of rage. He played games constantly. Gaming came before sleep, food, family, and friends. Gaming was *the* activity of Andy's life.

He bounced back and forth between his parents' separate homes until his mother refused to let him come back unless he agreed to some basic ground rules. Her boyfriend, a retired police officer, was no one to mess with. Backed by her boyfriend's unwavering support, Barb enforced a program of tough love. Andy was given a list of rules:

1. Absolutely no video games in the house.
2. Absolutely no video game playing, both at home *and* away from home.
3. You must tell the truth all the time—no exceptions.
4. If you play a video game and come clean about it, you will be allowed to do a makeup. Lying and then coming clean does not count.

5. You will sleep in the room in the basement and must clean your area once a week.

6. If you eat dinner at home, you will do the dishes afterwards.

7. You must get your GED within six months.

8. You must do GED coursework every day for at least an hour.

9. You must look for a job every day until you find one.

10. You must find a job within one month and work at that job a minimum of twenty hours a week.

11. You must leave the house at 8:30 a.m. Monday through Friday when we leave for work and not return until we come back from work.

12. If *all* of these conditions are not met, you will be asked to leave and will have one week to vacate the premises.

13. You will be given two warnings. The third violation will result in your having to move out.

14. I will trust you, but I will also verify.

Barb checked in with me several times a week, and when Andy came to my house, I enforced the same rules. (Although I initially had worked with Andy as an ADHD coach, I ended up becoming a close family friend. Andy used to come over to help me with my ADHD study groups, which was really just a convenient excuse for him to hang out with me.) Everything seemed to go well for a few months. He showed proof that he had been working on his GED and managed after about a month to get a job at a fast-food restaurant.

About six weeks later, Barb began to discuss Andy's finances with him and asked what he had done with his money. He said he had opened a bank account. Pursuant to her "trust, but verify" approach, she asked for proof. Andy said, "I didn't save any of the paperwork, but I'll get my statement soon, and then I can show you." He seemed proud of finally having his own bank account.

Something in his demeanor, however, activated Barb's motherly radar. She called me, somewhat panicked, because she felt something just wasn't right. She seemed angry because she felt that he was playing her for the fool. She asked me to look into the situation because she felt too stressed to maintain objectivity.

I posed as a counselor from a local community college and called the restaurant that employed Andy to ask the manager to verify his employment. The manager told me that Andy had been working but hadn't shown up for work in the past week. Another employee had told the manager that he'd seen Andy at GameStop, a used video game store.

I drove to the store and described Andy to the workers. "Oh, you mean Nintendo 64 spaz boy," one worker said in an irritated way. "He's been here from open to close for the past week and has come in four to five times a week for a while now." Andy's hyperactive, video-game-obsessed personality grated on most people, so he was hard to forget. I learned that Andy had been leading a secret video game life and that several younger kids came to the store regularly to watch his amazing play in certain Nintendo 64 games. They also told me that he had purchased a handheld Game Boy video game system along with several games.

Barb was crushed. She had been regularly searching his room and couldn't figure out where he had been hiding the Game Boy. Then she and I discovered a cubby hole in the drop-down ceiling of the basement. We lifted up one of the tiles and the Game Boy fell out. Barb started to cry, but decided to give Andy one more chance.

She gave him the opportunity to come clean when he came home that evening. "Are you sure you've been telling me everything?" she questioned him. "Yeah, I've been following all the rules," he replied indignantly. Barb responded, "Come clean with me now, or you may have to leave." He didn't budge, and when we shared the evidence with him, he flew into a rage about how we had no right to go behind his back and how we were out to get him.

Barb followed through on her tough love approach and kicked

Andy out. Unfortunately, several relatives tried to help Andy, continuing the cycle of enabling. As of six months ago, he had exhausted all family and friends. The last I heard, he was in California and being evicted from his apartment.

For parents with a child like Andy, sometimes tough love is necessary, and when, as a parent, you take that path, you must realize that your child may have to endure some rough patches before he or she is eventually willing to deal with the addiction. Some addicts have a lot farther to fall than others before they hit bottom. As a parent, you may have to let your child fall, and you may have to realize that the addiction is something within him or her and over which you ultimately have little control. You are not a failure as a parent if you cannot get your child to confront the addiction. Remember, it is embedded deep within the circuitry of the brain.

It is much easier to deal with this problem when your child is young, but regardless of age, most kids will try to find ways around your efforts at curtailment.

DECEPTION AND CONCEALMENT

Like Andy, your child will probably try to foil the system. Almost all kids do. One particularly crafty fourteen-year-old developed an elaborate plan to deceive his parents. He had been playing four to six hours of video games a day and had consistently circumvented his parents' attempts to curtail his play. They brought him to me, ostensibly because of his low grades, but I realized video games were a significant hurdle we had to overcome.

The full extent of the child's covert operation shocked me, but I was equally impressed at the workings of an inventive mind. James created several email accounts that had teachers' names in the addresses, thus creating the appearance of legitimacy. He began sending emails to his parents from these phony addresses, conveying some problems he was having in school. I am sure that he knew that his parents were less likely to be suspicious of bad news from school. He wrote the first email "from his counselor" and informed his folks:

Dear Mr. and Mrs. Johnson,

James has had some low test grades in Math and English, and we are worried about his performance. He needs to keep up with assignments and study for tests and quizzes. I will be regularly informing you of his progress. Please feel free to contact me with any questions you may have.

Predictably, James's parents sat him down and had a serious talk. This event occurred soon after they had started a video game reward system. James's father used this occasion to add a few reward possibilities, one of which tied eight hours of video game play on weekends to a positive report from his counselor.

From that point on until his ruse was discovered, James sent glowing emails to his parents every Friday from his counselor's fake email address. The phrases "amazing progress," "great focus," and "turned over a new leaf" found their way into the young man's fake emails. He sent other emails from his teachers that talked of As on tests and great classroom behavior—all of which, of course, added more game time.

The gig would have been up at parent–teacher conferences, except James sent an email to his parents "from his counselor" informing them that the conferences had been cancelled and would be rescheduled.

His father had actually been looking forward to conferences because it looked like they would be positive for a change. He wanted to hear how his son was finally living up to his potential. He eventually called the counselor to request a face-to-face meeting and learned quickly that he had been deceived by his son.

I believe that at this point, James had already crossed the line into video game addiction.

James's parents added up all of James's fraudulently obtained game time. They took away his game system and installed a lock box on his computer, limiting him to ten minutes a day so that he could check his email and for homework on teachers' Web sites. To have game time reinstated, James had to pay back all of his unearned game time, times two. This amounted to more than one hundred and fifty hours. It took him three months to dig himself out of the hole. His parents now use the method that Ronald Reagan used with Mikhail Gorbachev and the Soviet Union: "Trust, but verify."

Helping Cyber Addicts with Asperger's, ADHD, and Other Comorbidities

"It seems that for success in science or art, a dash of autism is essential. For success, the necessary ingredient may be an ability to turn away from the everyday world, from the simply practical, an ability to re-think a subject with originality so as to create in new, untrodden ways."
—Hans Asperger

People who struggle with cyber addiction often have other issues just below the surface. In many cases the excessive cyber use or gaming has led to a psychological evaluation that spotted other underlying issues. It is crucial that parents, professionals, and loved ones do not view video gaming addiction in a vacuum. It may be just half of the problem.

What this means is that when you move to help someone with a cyber addiction, it's important to consider other factors that may be involved in the person's use.

ASPERGER'S SYNDROME

Parents of kids with Asperger's syndrome (AS), a high-functioning form of autism, should use great caution when granting video game and computer access. With AS kids whose main interest is video games, parents often struggle getting them to focus on anything else. Many of the parents I work with have had good luck with daily video game reward systems (like the one I describe in James's story) with their AS children. The rewards definitely have to be daily with AS kids. Target behaviors should be very specific. AS children often need things spelled out in specific detail. Weekly recap meetings are also useful. Such meetings are used to assess the success of achieving target positive behaviors from the previous week.

Eliminating computers and video games completely is always an option, but parents taking such a path should be forewarned that it is incredibly difficult to keep any child isolated from electronics in today's world. Again, I advocate teaching responsible gaming.

ATTENTION-DEFICIT/HYPERACTIVITY DISORDER

If you have a child with ADHD who also games excessively, keep in mind that you are likely dealing with an innate predisposition towards addictive behavior. Therapy, coaching, and behavior modification strategies should be considered. On the other hand, if you have an excessive gamer, consider that ADHD may be involved. Most of the ADHD kids I see in my professional practice as an ADHD coach are also excessive gamers. They likewise also have troubles with the cyber world all across the board, whether it be with Facebook, MySpace, excessive video viewing, pornography, or their iPhones. Incidentally, cell phones are one of the most powerful rewards that actually motivate individuals with ADHD. Treat them as a privilege.

BIPOLAR DISORDER

The bipolar folks I have worked with have had a penchant for darker types of video games and three-quarters of them were full-fledged World of Warcraft addicts. I bring this issue up to highlight the importance of viewing video gaming addiction and excessive Internet use as possible signs of deeper issues. This reality underscores the importance of seeking professional help. In addition, I have had several folks who came to see me with the diagnosis of ADHD who later turned out to be bipolar. This is a somewhat common misdiagnosis in folks who later are found to have bipolar disorder.

If you have a video gamer who seems to really merge with the games and has significant disruptions and distortions in sleep patterns, consider that some serious issues in addition to addiction may be at work.

COADDICTION

It should come as no surprise that, since addicts generally have cerebral hardwiring that predisposes them to addiction, folks who are addicted to the cyber world are also at risk for substance abuse in addition to other behavioral addictions. I have had many cyber addicts come to me who were also habitual marijuana users. In some cases, marijuana was used to enhance the level of connectedness with the game, or to make the escape to the Internet a more fulfilling experience. Substance abuse and cyber addiction often go hand in hand. Coaddictions represent a very complicated situation, one in which professional support absolutely must be sought.

COMPUTER ADEPTS

At fourteen, James possessed a high degree of electronic sophistication. He used all of his genius, however, to excel at computer games and to cover up his addictive behavior. Games gave James a satisfaction that he could not find anywhere else. "He gravitated toward computers from the time he was a baby," his mother told me. "We just never realized that could lead to problems."

Jake, the young man who joined the Army to quell his video game addiction, urges parents with kids like James to "get their computer-oriented children into computer classes and camps at an early age." He believes such measures will prevent serious problems from developing. "These kids need to know that they not only have valuable skills, but that they are valuable as people," Jake says. "I never knew I was valuable, and I wasted years of my life feeling miserable and being glued to a computer screen."

Look for summer classes at local high schools, community

colleges, and universities. Computer camps for kids abound. (See "Resources" for a few recommendations and notes on how to start the process of finding an appropriate camp.) You can enroll your child in camps that specialize in networking, servers, programming, Web site design, and yes, even video game design and development. Video game design, by the way, is a great way to hook young people into math and science. You will be ensuring that your child develops self-esteem, has opportunities to socialize with like-minded individuals, and even builds marketable skills. If you have a computer-oriented child, remember what Jake said: "The world needs people like us!"

Knowledge, Support, and Action

Having read this book, you have armed yourself with a great deal of information about cyber addictions. Again, before you attempt to use any of this information to help a loved one, it is crucial to establish a support network. Ideally, you will consult with a professional (therapist, social worker, addiction counselor, addiction specialist) to help ascertain any possible underlying issues that need to be addressed with your loved one, as well as to examine your own issues that might get in the way of you being effective. In addition, a network of close friends and family members also plays a critical role in you maintaining your own emotional equilibrium, and can be great sounding boards through which to test your ideas and appraisal of the situation. Twelve Step support groups such as Al-Anon are quite useful as well. Once you have your team members together, it is time to make use of them to come up with your plan of action based on the intricacies of your addicted loved one's situation.

Remember, addiction is an insidious condition, one especially prone to relapse. You can control your choices, but you cannot control those of your addicted loved one. Expect setbacks and realize that one piece of success may be quickly followed by failure. It will be important for you to heed the age-old wisdom: "Let go and let God" (as you understand God).

resources

Inpatient Treatment Facilities

The following inpatient facilities in the United States have extensive experience with Internet and video game addictions. They have all recently received a good deal of positive media attention. No client of mine has ever been admitted at these facilities, but I have heard good things from colleagues about their results.

Illinois Institute for Addiction Recovery
5409 N. Knoxville Ave.
Peoria, IL 61614
Phone: 800-522-3784
Web site: www.addictionrecov.org

Center for Internet Addiction
P.O. Box 72
Bradford, PA 16701
Phone: 814-451-2405
Web site: http://netaddiction.com

reSTART Internet Addiction Recovery Program
1001 290th Ave. SE
Fall City, WA 98024-7403
Phone: 425-417-1715
Web site: www.netaddictionrecovery.com

Outdoor Programs

Outward Bound
This organization's programs teach problem-solving, setting goals, and interpersonal communication—all skills that many cyber addicts lack. Total isolation from electronics gives participants space to reflect on their lives. The program also encourages

them to find a way to contribute to their communities and make a difference in the world.

Web site: www.outwardbound.org
Contact: 845-424-4000

Aspen Education Group (AEG)
A therapeutic wilderness training program, Aspen Education Group (AEG) has extensive experience dealing with video-game-addicted teens. In recent years, AEG has been experiencing a huge influx of young people who are checking out of life, refusing to go to school, and engaging in obsessive cyber activities.

Web site: www.aspeneducation.com
Contact: 888-972-7736

There are many similar wilderness programs that can be found easily on the Internet. I list Aspen because of my positive experiences with this organization. If you choose to explore these programs, make sure to choose one experienced specifically with cyber addictions.

Computer and Video Game Camps

WHAT TO LOOK FOR IN A CAMP

A simple Google search using the key phrase "Computer Camps," will bring up hundreds of entries. As you sift through these, you should pay attention to a variety of factors to ensure that your child will be safe, has a good experience, and comes out with a set of skills that can be practiced and honed. Ideally, you start off with more basic camps, and when your child has a good experience, he or she will be willing to try the more intense and specialized camps. There are simple factors you can watch out for that will contribute to a positive experience.

The most important attribute is that the camp is age appropriate. I have had some parents find their sixteen- and seventeen-year-olds what they thought to be great camps. When the teens arrived, they discovered that they were three to four years older than most of the other campers and, as a result, felt out of place. If you have a thirteen-year-old, make sure that the majority of the kids in his or her program are between twelve and fourteen. This same logic applies to children of any age.

Most parents of computer-adept children do not have the knowledge to fully appreciate their child's skills. Thus, it can be quite difficult to navigate through the countless options displayed on a Google search. It can be very helpful to talk to the computer teacher at school to determine what your child's knowledge level is so that you can gauge the most appropriate placement level. You may have a friend who is an Information Technology specialist who would be able to assist you. You have to accurately assess the child's skill level in order to find a good fit for a computer camp, and you may need help to do this.

When you find some camps that you think would help your child, take a few minutes and search through their Web sites. Look at the pictures that are displayed. Are the children in those pictures similar in age to yours? Do they look like the kinds of kids your child would connect with? Look over the programs that are offered and then bring in your child. See what he or she thinks. I had a sixteen-year-old young man whose parents suggested it was a good idea for him to attend a computer camp. He was vehemently opposed to the idea until he spent some time at one of my study groups. I asked him for his input in trying to pick out a computer camp for another young man. In this process, he found some that actually interested him. Make your child a part of the process. I find that it is easier to pique their interest when I talk about fun activities such as network gaming parties and 3-D design classes that many camps offer. Get on their level and engage them.

If you have a few serious options, the next step is to call people at the camp. Remember: they make more money when they have more kids. I have called the same camps at different times and given different age and computer-skill level criteria. Some camps' representatives were honest and said their camp is perhaps not the best fit. In about 50 percent of the camps that I called, however, no matter what criteria I gave, those representatives said their camp was a "great fit!" I caution you to be aware of these facts and, if possible, get the names and contact information of young people who have attended the camp (perhaps their parents contact information as well) and interview them. You can really get a sense of the types of young people the camp caters to by talking with former campers.

I do not endorse any computer camps and urge parents to do their own research. I have, however, listed a few below that I think are worth checking out. I cannot endorse these camps because an appropriate fit depends on a lot of factors unique to each child. Parents are the best judge of what camps work best for their children. Please do some extensive research before picking a camp. Your child's future could very well depend on the thoroughness and care you bring to this process.

SummerTech

Of all the computer and video game camp folks I have talked with, the person who impressed me the most was Steven Fink at SummerTech. SummerTech focuses on the whole experience. The camp is focused on having kids grow emotionally, in addition to tuning up and adding to their computer skills. Staff members are trained to be aware of the camper's needs, both emotionally and intellectually. Many of the staff are former campers who have returned. They teach computer programming, animation, Web design, music, and moviemaking. They work on the premise that what the campers learn is only part of the experience. They're always on the lookout for a challenge.

SummerTech is the only children's program in the world I have found that teaches Machinima. Machinima is a medium of moviemaking using 3-D virtual worlds and other video games. The campers use this technology to create their own stories. Many of these campers' films have been seen in the Machinima Film Festival in New York.

Web site: http://summertech.net
Contact: Steven Fink, 866-814-TECH (8324)

Game Camp USA

Game Camp USA is an academic summer camp that teaches middle and high school students how to build their own video games. Game Camp's program uses kids' natural affinity for gaming to encourage an active interest in education, particularly in art, math, and computer science. The students code the logic for their games in a contemporary programming language (currently Java or C#). Breaks for gaming and swimming are also included during the day, and camp-wide gaming tournaments are available in the evening. Weeklong and weekend, day, and overnight sessions are available each summer at various locations throughout the United States. If there is a Game Camp USA near you, this can be a more affordable option than many of the other camps I have encountered because you will not have to pay for room and board.

Web site: www.gamecamp.com
Contact: 888-663-9633

National Computer Camps

Now in its thirty-first year, National Computer Camps (NCC) is one of the oldest computer camps in the United States. The focus of NCC is 2-D and 3-D video game design, computer programming, digital video production, Web page design, A+ and Network+ certification, and software applications including animation, Flash, and graphics. An optional sports program is also available. Campers may attend one or multiweek sessions with a continuous curriculum that is age appropriate and suitable for beginners to super-advanced. The camps work well for both experienced and first-time campers.

The camp has a wide variety of options for course work. Michael Zabinski, the camp's director, has a great passion for helping video game–oriented kids turn their interest in gaming into a set of marketable skills.

Web site: www.nccamp.com
Contact: Michael Zabinski, Ph.D., 203-710-5771

notes

Chapter 1: Welcome to the Cyber Universe

1. Douglas Gentile, "Pathological Video Game Use among Youth 8 to 18: A National Study," *Psychological Science* 20, no. 5 (2009): 594–602.
2. Lea Goldman, "This Is Your Brain on Clicks," *Forbes* 175, no. 10 (May 9, 2005): 54.
3. D. H. Ahn, "Korean Policy on Treatment and Rehabilitation for Adolescents' Internet Addiction," *2007 International Symposium on the Counseling and Treatment of Youth Internet Addiction. Seoul, Korea* (National Youth Commission, 2007), 49.
4. The National Institute on Media and the Family, "MediaWise Video Game and Computer Game Report Card: A Ten Year Overview," August 1, 2007, http://mediafamily.org/research/report_10yr_overview.shtml.
5. Entertainment Software Association, "Essential Facts about the Computer and Video Game Industry: 2007 Sales, Demographic and Usage Data," August 22, 2007, www.theesa.com/facts/pdfs/ESA_EF_2007.pdf.
6. Ibid.
7. UN News Centre, "Number of Cell Phone Subscribers to Hit 4 Billion This Year, UN Says," September 25, 2008, www.un.org/apps/news/story.asp?NewsID=28251.
8. Internet World Stats, "Internet Usage Statistics: The Internet Big Picture: World Internet Users and Population Stats," www.internetworldstats.com/stats.htm.
9. Nick Burcher, "Latest Facebook Usage Statistics by Country: 12 Months of Extraordinary Global Growth," www.nickburcher.com/2009/07/latest-facebook-usage-statistics-by.html.
10. Anderson Analytics, "Social Network Study Profiles Special Network Users on Facebook, MySpace, LinkedIn and Twitter," June 13, 2009, www.marketresearchworld.net/index.php?option=com_content&task=view&id=2675&Itemid=77.
11. John Luo, "The Facebook Phenomenon: Boundaries and Controversies," *Primary Psychiatry* 16, no. 11 (2009): 19.

12. Korina Lopez, "It's a State of Mind, Not a Place," *USA Today*, August 26, 2009.
13. James Brightman, "Study: Video Game Addiction Similar to Asperger's," Game Daily, April 3, 2008, http://asdgestalt.com/viewtopic.php?f=23&t=2090.
14. Timothy E. Wilens, "When AD/HD and Substance Abuse Collide," *The New CHADD Information and Resource Guide to AD/HD* (Washington, DC: National Resource Center on AD/HD, 2006), 89–92.
15. Edward M. Hallowell and John J. Ratey, *Driven to Distraction*, 1st ed. (New York: Touchstone, 1994).
16. Verena Dobnik, "Surgeons May Err Less by Playing Video Games," April 7, 2004, www.msnbc.msn.com/id/4685909.
17. Howard Witt and *Chicago Tribune*, "I Told You to Play Your Video Game! Studies Find Educational Benefits," *The Record* (Bergen County, NJ), February 15, 2007.
18. J. E. Driskell and D. J. Dwyer, "Microcomputer Videogame Based Training," *Educational Technology* 24, no. 2 (1984): 11–16.
19. Pamela M. Kato, Steve W. Cole, Veronica M. Marin-Bowling, Gary V. Dahl, and Brad H. Pollock, "Controlled Trial of a Video Game to Improve Health Related Outcomes Among Adolescents and Young Adults with Cancer," Hope Lab, March 2006, www.hopelab.org/wp-content/uploads/2007/12/SBM_DataPoster.pdf.
20. International Business Machines (IBM) and Seriosity.com, "Virtual Worlds, Real Leaders: Online Games Put the Future of Business Leadership on Display," September 23, 2007, www.seriosity.com/downloads/GIO_PDF_web.pdf.
21. Ibid.
22. Valerie Barker, "Older Adolescents' Motivations for Social Network Site Use: The Influence of Gender, Group Identity, and Collective Self-Esteem," *CyberPsychology & Behavior* (2009): 213.
23. Nicole Ellison, Charles Steinfield, and Cliff Lampe, "The Benefits of Facebook 'Friends': Social Capital and College Students' Use of Online Social Network Sites," *Journal of Computer-Mediated Communication* 12, no. 3 (2006): 444.

Chapter 2: Choose Your Poison

1. "Twitter versus Facebook," January 13, 2009, www.twitip.com/twitter-versus-facebook.
2. Ibid.
3. Ayiti: The Cost of Life was put together by high school students in cooperation with GameLab. You can view the game at www.unicef.org/voy/explore/rights/explore_3142.html.
4. Jagex Software, "Advertisers," November 3, 2007, www.jagex.com/corporate/Advertisers/general.ws.

Chapter 3: Your Brain in Cyberland

1. Alan Leshner, "Addiction Is a Brain Disease, and It Matters," *Science* 278 (October 3, 1997): 45–47.
2. M. J. Koepp, R. N. Gunn, A. D. Lawrence, V. J. Cunningham, A. Dagher, T. Jones, D. J. Brooks, C. J. Bench, and P. M. Grasby, "Evidence for Striatal Dopamine Release During a Video Game," *Nature* 393 (May 21, 1998): 266–68.
3. Lisa N. Legrand, William G. Iacono, and Matt McGue, "Predicting Addiction: Behavioral Genetics Uses Twins and Time to Decipher the Origins of Addiction and Learn Who Is Most Vulnerable," *American Scientist* (March–April 2005): 140–47.
4. Chih-Hung Ko, Gin-Chung Liu, Sigmund Hsiao, Ju-Yu Yen, Ming-Jen Yang, Wei-Chen Lin, Cheng-Fang Yen, Cheng-Sheng Chen, "Brain Activities Associated with Gaming Urge of Online Gaming Addiction," *Journal of Psychiatric Research* 43, no. 7 (April 2009): 746.
5. Constance Holden, "Behavioral Addictions: Do They Exist?" *Science* (November 2, 2001): 980–82.
6. Leshner, "Addiction Is a Brain Disease," 45–47.
7. James D. Stoehr, *The Neurobiology of Addiction*, 1st ed. (Philadelphia: Chelsea House, 2006), 22–23, 93.
8. Eric J. Nestler and George K. Aghajanian, "Molecular and Cellular Basis of Addiction," *Science* (October 3, 1997): 58–63.
9. Ibid.
10. Véronique Deroche-Gamonet, David Belin, and Pier Piazza, "Evidence for Addiction-like Behavior in the Rat," *Science* (August 13, 2004): 1014–17.

11. Leshner, "Addiction Is a Brain Disease," 45; Stoehr, *The Neurobiology of Addiction*, 22–23, 93.
12. Stoehr, *The Neurobiology of Addiction*.
13. Leshner, "Addiction Is a Brain Disease," 46.
14. Ibid.
15. Ibid.
16. Ibid.
17. Ibid.
18. Holden, "Behavioral Addictions: Do They Exist?" 981.
19. Ibid.
20. Jennifer L. Powers, "Dopamine," in *Chemistry: Foundations and Applications*, vol. 2, ed. J. J. Lagowski (New York: Macmillan Reference USA, 2004), 22–23.
21. Ronald A. Ruden, *The Craving Brain*, 2nd ed. (New York: Harper Collins, 1997), 18–19.
22. "Brain Activity in Overeaters Similar to Drug Addicts," *ASRT Scanner* 25, no. 1 (June 2007).
23. Gene-Jack Wang, "New Food-Addiction Link Found," Brookhaven National Laboratory, May 20, 2002, www.bnl.gov/bnlweb/pubaf/pr/2002/bnlpr052002.htm.
24. Steven Johnson, "Your Brain on Video Games," *Discover* 26, no. 7 (July 24, 2005).
25. Ibid.
26. Koepp, "Evidence for Striatal Dopamine Release," 266–68.
27. Ibid.
28. J. Michael Bostwick and Jeffrey A. Bucci, *Mayo Clinic Proceedings* 83, no. 2 (February 2008): 226.
29. R. Thalemann, K. Wölfling, and S. M. Grüsser, "Specific Cue Reactivity on Computer Game-related Cues in Excessive Gamers," *Behavioral Neuroscience*, 121, no. 3 (June 2007): 614–18.
30. Ibid.
31. Stoehr, *The Neurobiology of Addiction*, 20–22, 93.
32. Joseph Biederman, Michael C. Monuteaux, Thomas Spencer, Timothy E. Wilens, Heather A. MacPherson, Stephen V. Faraone, "Stimulant Therapy and Risk for Subsequent Substance Use Disorders in Male Adults with ADHD: A Naturalistic Controlled 10-Year Follow-Up Study," *American Journal of Psychiatry* 165, no. 5 (May 2008): 597–603.

33. Yen Ju-Yu, Cheng-Fang Yen, Cheng-Sheng Chen, Tze-Chun Tang, Chih-Hung Ko, "The Association between Adult ADHD Symptoms and Internet Addiction among College Students: The Gender Difference," *CyberPsychology & Behavior* 12, no. 2 (April 2009): 187.

34. Stoehr, *The Neurobiology of Addiction*, 67.

35. Ibid.

36. Young Sik Lee, Doug Hyun Han, Kevin C. Yang, Melissa A. Daniels, Chul Na, Baik Seok Kee, Perry F. Renshaw, "Depression like Characteristics of 5HTTLPR Polymorphism and Temperament in Excessive Internet Users," *Journal of Affective Disorders* 109, no. 1 (July 2008): 168.

37. Ibid.

38. Legrand, "Predicting Addiction," 140–47 (see chap. 3, n. 3).

39. Ibid.

40. John Hoffman and Susan Froemke, eds., *Addiction: Why Can't They Just Stop?* (New York: Rodale, 2007), 64.

41. Ruden, *The Craving Brain*, 18–19.

42. Ibid.

43. Ruden, *The Craving Brain*, 50.

44. Michael D. Lemonick, "The Science of Addiction," *Time* 170, no. 3 (July 16, 2007): 42–48.

45. Laura Helmuth, "Addiction: Beyond the Pleasure Principle," *Science* 294, no. 5544 (November 2, 2001): 983–84.

46. M. J. Christie, "Cellular Neuroadaptations to Chronic Opioids: Tolerance Withdrawal and Addiction," *British Journal of Pharmacology* 154, no. 2 (May 2008): 384–96.

Chapter 4: Into the Black Hole

1. Bill Asenjo and Teresa G. Odle, "Addiction," *Gale Encyclopedia of Medicine* (Detroit, MI: Thomson Gale, 2004).

2. Ibid.

3. Kimberly Young, "Addiction to MMORPGs: Symptoms and Treatment," Center for Internet Addiction Recovery, 2006, www.netaddiction.com/articles/addiction_to_mmorpgs.pdf.

4. Liz Woolley has a list of warning signs at Online Gamers Anonymous (www.olganonboard.org). Conversations with Liz helped me in formalizing my own list

5. Darko Hinič, Goran Mihajlovič, Željko Špirič, Slavica Đukič-Dejanovič, and Mirjana Jovanovič, "Excessive Internet Use—Addiction Disorder or Not?" *Vojnosanitetski Pregled: Military Medical & Pharmaceutical Journal of Serbia & Montenegro* 65, no. 10 (October 2008): 766.

6. Ibid.

7. I owe this description to David P., a member of one of my recovery groups. He gave me great insight into the mindset surrounding MMORPGs. His candid and revealing personal story gave me much-needed insight into aspects of the video game world with which I was unfamiliar.

8. Sid Meier, *Civilization Manual*, Civilization Fanatics, 2000, www.civfanatics.com/civ1/manual/civ1_man.htm#2a.

9. Ibid.

10. Kwisook Choi, Hyunsook Son, Myunghee Park, Jinkyu Han, Kitai Kim, Byungkoo Lee, and Hyesun Gwak, "Internet Overuse and Excessive Daytime Sleepiness in Adolescents," *Psychiatry & Clinical Neurosciences* 63, no. 4 (August 2009): 455.

11. "Death Linked to EverQuest," August 10, 2003, www.sfsignal.com/archives/000083.html.

12. These postings are not direct quotes, but rather my synthesis of many postings I have read and anecdotes clients have shared with me. I did this to protect privacy.

13. Timothy E. Wilens, "When AD/HD and Substance Abuse Collide," *The New CHADD Information and Resource Guide to AD/HD* (Washington, DC: National Resource Center on AD/HD, 2006), 89–92.

14. Young Sik Lee, "Depression like Characteristics," 165 (see chap. 3, n. 36).

15. *Age of Empires Manual* (Microsoft, 1997).

Chapter 5: Climbing Out of the Hole

1. John Bradshaw, *Healing the Shame That Binds You* (Deerfield Beach, FL: Health Communications, 1998), 40.

Chapter 6: The Journey of Recovery Continues

1. "Gratitude Is Good Medicine for Organ Recipients," August 16, 2007, www.sciencedaily.com/releases/2007/08/070815135030.htm.
2. Ibid.
3. Mark Strassmann, "Uncle Sam Wants Video Gamers," CBS News, February 8, 2005, www.cbsnews.com/stories/2005/02/08/eveningnews/main672455.shtml.
4. "America's Army Game Features," America's Army: The Official Army Game, United States Army, 2008, http://forum.americasarmy.com/viewtopic.php?t=271086.
5. This story was corroborated using several sources.
6. "America's Army Medic Training Helps Save a Life," America's Army: The Official Army Game, United States Army, 2008, http://forum.americasarmy.com/viewtopic.php?t=271086.
7. The model I follow for groups was pioneered by my friend Bill Kauth. His book, *A Circle of Men* (New York: St. Martin's Press, 1992), has been an invaluable resource for me over the years.
8. "Addicted: Suicide over EverQuest?" CBS News: 48 Hours, October 18, 2002, www.cbsnews.com/stories/2002/10/17/48hours/main525965.shtml.
9. Roger Collier, "Virtual Detox: Inpatient Therapy for Internet Addicts," *Canadian Medical Association Journal* 181, no. 9 (October 27, 2009): E193–E194.

Chapter 7: A Guide for Loved Ones

1. "About Outward Bound," February 14, 2008, www.outwardbound.org/aboutus.vp.html.

About the Author

Kevin Roberts is a recovering video game addict who runs support groups to help cyber addicts who struggle to get their lives back on track. He is a nationally recognized expert on video gaming addiction and a regular conference speaker. His background is in education, and for the last eleven years he has been an academic coach, helping folks dealing with attention-deficit/hyperactivity disorder succeed in school and life. He is the curriculum developer and a board member of the EmpowerADD Project, which uses a sixteen-module program that is designed to give individuals with ADHD the skills they need to succeed.

Kevin speaks many foreign languages fluently and performs stand-up comedy at conferences and conventions. He is presently putting the finishing touches on a one-man show about his life. He speaks around the country about cyber addiction and ADHD.

Hazelden, a national nonprofit organization founded in 1949, helps people reclaim their lives from the disease of addiction. Built on decades of knowledge and experience, Hazelden offers a comprehensive approach to addiction that addresses the full range of patient, family, and professional needs, including treatment and continuing care for youth and adults, research, higher learning, public education and advocacy, and publishing.

A life of recovery is lived "one day at a time." Hazelden publications, both educational and inspirational, support and strengthen lifelong recovery. In 1954, Hazelden published *Twenty-Four Hours a Day,* the first daily meditation book for recovering alcoholics, and Hazelden continues to publish works to inspire and guide individuals in treatment and recovery, and their loved ones. Professionals who work to prevent and treat addiction also turn to Hazelden for evidence-based curricula, informational materials, and videos for use in schools, treatment programs, and correctional programs.

Through published works, Hazelden extends the reach of hope, encouragement, help, and support to individuals, families, and communities affected by addiction and related issues.

For questions about Hazelden publications,
please call **800-328-9000**
or visit us online at **hazelden.org/bookstore.**